Developing Critical Youth Work Theory

Building Professional Judgment in the Community Context

Brian Belton
YMCA George Williams College

SENSE PUBLISHERS
ROTTERDAM/BOSTON/TAIPEI

A C.I.P. record for this book is available from the Library of Congress.

ISBN 978-90-8790-943-7 (paperback)
ISBN 978-90-8790-944-4 (hardback)
ISBN 978-90-8790-945-1 (e-book)

Published by: Sense Publishers,
P.O. Box 21858, 3001 AW
Rotterdam, The Netherlands
http://www.sensepublishers.com

Printed on acid-free paper

TABLE OF CONTENTS

INTRODUCTION

I set goals, take control, drink out my own bottle
I make mistakes but learn from every one
And when it's said and done
I bet this brother be a better one
If I upset you don't stress
Never forget, that God isn't finished with me yet

–Tupac Shakur

This book sets out to be critical of the theory, practice, language and policy of youth work in the context of community education. At the same time it will examine and problematise the practice environment; land, place, locale, attitude, and condition which have come to be known collectively as 'community'.

It is not my intention to put right various wrongs, or to critique for the sake of it. Youth work has failed to gain the status its practitioners deserve for two main reasons. Firstly it has not been served well in terms of critical theory. Secondly – and as a consequence – it has largely failed to facilitate the honing of professional judgement. Youth work is in danger of becoming a craft, following various versions of the same set of instructions that can more or less be identified in most of the literature relating to the profession.

During the contemporary period, informal education has attempted to step into this breach in the foundations of youth work. However, as one trawls though the writing relating to it, the shoals of 'shoulds' and 'musts' might cause anyone weaned on the custom and practice of youth work to despair. Traditionally youth workers devoted themselves to working with others to find pathways in life through taking chances and opportunities for themselves. Hence, from a very long list of precepts, telling youth workers to educate young people (who have not asked to be educated) while insisting, for instance, that we should '*make compassion the kernel*' of our work, all the time promoting a rather vague notion of democracy, is both prescriptive and confused.

If we are giving people stuff they have not asked for, and making ourselves operate to a prescribed attitude and conduct of informal education, how is it democratic? This is not what we have sought to do in terms of best practice in youth work; it is the diametrical opposite. How can we develop as a largely non-directive, but developmental, force in the life of society if we are to adhere to a collection of one-size-fits-all, formulaic coaching schedules, set-in-stone codes and apparently unquestionable rules? I am not talking about health and safety issues, nor child protection procedures, but maxims like 'I must never impose my opinion on young people'. Most young people I have known have not treated me or many other adults as a voice that must be followed – often very much the contrary. Another often recited mantra is, 'I never encourage dependence'. However, the act of insisting on independence is in fact dependent on that assertion. Someone supposedly working on someone else for them not to be dependent is a contradiction in terms.

Statements of this type are premised on deficit models, which I will expand on below, and simple professional ego. For example, to imply young people have no choice what to do once I've given my opinion is to see them both as dependent and in deficit with regard to making up their own mind. But are people under a certain age, 16, 18, 21, that malleable? Such deficit perspectives also imply that people are looking for any and every opportunity to be dependent, which again is something not really understood as a common trait among teenagers and those in their early twenties.

What follows is not so much an instruction manual but analysis, views, narrative, critique, discussion that includes, most importantly perhaps, thoughtful contemplation of and deliberation on 'real life' experience and practice. This has been achieved via an eclectic and lively mix of perspectives that embraces academic, practitioner and journalistic contributions reflecting on social, economic, political and historical considerations.

The book uses several recurring themes. Prominent among these are deficit awareness and related colonial attitudes. I have also consistently reminded the reader of the capitalist social and economic structure within which youth work is framed and formed, and which it confirms, and what Foucault calls the 'Carceral'; the idea that society as is effectively a reflection of the prison. Public space is transformed into defendable space, dominated by forms of surveillance and control mechanisms. Such social environmental considerations are mostly ignored in much of the literature relating to youth work and informal education perhaps because these are stark foundations. But they provide a firm footing on which to develop strategies and professional judgment for meaningful practice that has impact and purpose. We are more secure and potentially more effective starting from a point that resembles where we are, rather than setting up practice direction from where we wish we could be.

This stance is not about conjuring up good guys and bad guys, and bears no resemblance to conspiracy theories. However, I am implicating the nature of social formation into analysis – the structure, process and dynamics of society. Geoffrey Kay and James Mott set a standard for this in the 20th century context in their concise epic *Political Order and the Law of Labour* (MacMillan, 1982). I have attempted to set out a continuous sociological and political theme that understands, for example, that although politicians might well have every good intention in framing legislation, the character of society, its networks and mechanics, will cause the effects of the same to follow a number of logical, although not always straightforwardly predictable, channels. These conduits are shaped by social conditions, power relations, authority structures and historical influences, the likes of which Foucault, Fanon and others have confronted, deciphered, deconstructed and critiqued. Overall, this book, embracing this tradition, provides a determined, sociologically analytical perspective that offers a novel critical response to youth work within community education practice that energises and provokes the development of professional judgement.

What follows is designed so that professional practitioners, and those training for the profession, might gain some means to initially question what passes for theory in the youth work/informal education realm. Within this an effort is made to justify the terms we use almost reactively, one of the basic characteristics of higher education. This is not done for its own sake, but to promote understanding of what our aims mean, and a consciousness of what it is we seek to do. This combined endeavour can be part of the means to produce much needed new theory for the individual development of professional judgement, finding pathways through taking chances and opportunities.

To quote Harry Batt an 11 year old I worked with in my first post after I qualified: 'Why should you do what anyone else tells you?' Why do they know better than you?' Not just good questions, but Harry may have possibly worked out a radical way of honing professional judgement. Much of what follows is based on this attitude using deconstructive logic, biography, practitioner consideration and analysis of practice and theory. Overall it provides what I think constitutes the first really close and critical look at some of the sometimes meaningless, terminology that infects youth work, its site of practice (the community) and the rhetoric of informal education.

I have tried to avoid pointless citation of much of the familiar literature. However, the more academically demanding analysis, for example, when referring to race and ethnicity, has necessarily included relevant references. In general I have tried not to write an entirely academic book as I want the work to fit in with professional needs, be accessible and quick to read. This said, most of what follows has been run by hundreds of undergraduate students in youth work and related fields and been usefully used by the same, so the work is track tested.

As a piece this book seeks to
- Question if community education is a viable framework for youth work practice
- Demonstrate that informal education is not an equivalent to, or replacement for, youth work, but a set of tools and precepts that youth workers have deployed which can be shown to be founded on anachronistic attitudes and as such redundant
- Provide the seeds of a new paradigm of youth work that while it might have educational impact, does not necessarily have straightforward educational outcomes
- Argue that youth work can be an enterprising and novel facility for 'world building' via the implication and embracing of the young as a source – and an inspiration for – social renewal, rather than as a population category that functions as a focal point of professional treatment
- Motivate questioning and critical approaches across the practice spectrum to generate clear professional judgement to enhance service delivery, quality of client experience and the production of policy that is both appropriate to society and pertinent to users.

The material also aims to politicise a group of professionals who have become almost terminally depoliticised through decades of surveillance and control-oriented policy from successive governments presiding over a society increasingly suspicious and fearful of it youth population. This politicisation includes definite strategies and tactics that can be implemented at individual, area and professional levels. This is not so much about accepting the manipulative role of agents of change, framed as that is in the conventions of promoting a non-politicised status quo, but offering a means to take on a responsibility as a vanguard in the socialisation of knowledge and meaningful social action. This is not strung around the deficit perception of 'personal development' or the illusion of 'community education' but a definite desire for pragmatic social development.

The logical premise of individual development is social development. Environments that inhibit social and political development restrict developmental room for the individual. This is not saying youth workers can change society, or should even try to, but it is suggesting that they can be part of the means to influence social reformation and a challenge authority structures. The Solidarity movement that arose in Poland in the 1980s was premised on ordinary working people creating enclaves of freedom within a State structure founded on 'unfreedom'. This developed into a framework of freedom throughout a whole population that eventually brought down a Soviet dominated government in an essentially non-violent way. Three months later, in November 1989, the Berlin wall was opened, the prelude to the erosion of the Iron Curtain and the demise of the USSR in 1991. This is a historically recent example of how people, when they become aware that authority taken by a minority is reliant on the majority giving up their authority, can take back that authority.

Youth workers know better than most that authority does not follow gravity, that this perception is the result of a sort of conjuring trick. Authority arises from the base of society. Youth workers are in what maybe an ideal position to demonstrate that via the pooling and processing of collective influence, authority can be made to push up from its actual roots.

Forms of instruction tend to introduce a series of ways of doing things that are comparatively easily to connect with what has been done before. This can be a comforting process wherein we can feel better equipped, having developed our expertise. But education is something a bit different from this. The expert, knowing how to do something, is not necessarily the most educated person in terms of intellect. When two or more people apply their intelligence to something disagreement is likely at some stage. This is not always a comfortable experience as it probably involves argument. If a person is not acclimatised to this the risk is that they may be offended by the process. However, as Black Panther Eldridge Cleaver had it, *Too much agreement kills the chat.*

It is probable that most discoveries of any significance, from the earth not being flat to genetic engineering, have caused at least somebody somewhere offence in that their beliefs and understandings have been questioned. Successful education, unlike instruction, has a relatively high chance of being recognised by the level of offence, objection and dissention it provokes. But if this can be embraced the turbulent experience of education can stoke and work with the imagination on to creating new and exciting possibilities. It was Albert Einstein who insisted that *Imagination is more important than knowledge. For knowledge is limited to all we now know and understand, while imagination embraces the entire world, and all there ever will be to know and understand.* That feels more a bit more alluring than, for example, merely looking over one's shoulder at what has happened in the past and applying that to the present and the immediate future, as if what 'is' is a mirror of what 'was'. The pubescent confusion of Alice as she ventured though the looking glass – 'reflecting-in-and-on-action'.

I know that these pages will not please some or indeed many readers. People sometimes like to be told what they already know rather than have well loved and nurtured ideas challenged or taken apart. I make no apology for not doing this. I, like most people, do not wish to be unpopular or to offend. But the more one's investment in a field, the more likely is the pain when that asset is depreciated. However, I would say that I have not set out to provide a 'balanced position'. As my first sociology teacher once said: 'Perhaps consider both sides of the coin, but particularly the other side.' This book is something of that other side, written from a background of 35 years in youth work as a practitioner, tutor, supervisor and lecturer. It is the fruit of contact with thousands of youth workers across the world and many more thousands of young people. These ideas have been more welcomed than spurred and are offered here not as the 'once and for all story' but as a means of redressing the balance – to say what many youth workers have wanted to say and for many reasons have not been able to. I trust they will be taken in the spirit of healthy questioning and an attempt to break a mould that I believe needs breaking. I'm not even sure that youth work can have a mould at all. It is a thing constantly in the making. That is what I aim to do and facilitate.

I don't mean to sound sleezy but tease me. I don't want it if it's that easy – Tupac Shakur

BIBLIOGRAPHY

Carroll, L., & Gardner, M. (Ed.). (1970). *The annotated Alice. Alice's adventures in Wonderland and through the looking-glass*. Penguin.

Cleaver, E. (1971). *Soul on ice*. Panther modern society.

Kay, G., & Mott, J. (1982). *Political order and the law of labour*. MacMillan.

CHAPTER 1

THE PARADOX OF COMMUNITY

The only thing that comes to a sleeping man is dreams

–Tupac Shakur

The community is often seen as the site of practice with young people – but where is it? Traditionally communities have been understood as having a geographical basis, such as a rural village or inner-city neighbourhood, but in the contemporary era community is not limited by geography. Communities can arise around common interests or identity, even be virtually based. Community doesn't even seem to be restricted by size as we now talk in terms of the 'national community', even the 'global community'. Community is everywhere and ever present. Disturbingly, anything that is everywhere is logically nowhere. If everything were white there would be no white. We can only call something white because some things are not white – comparatives are needed if particulars are to be identified. However, the number of books, articles and papers written about community incline one to believe it might be among the most thought about concepts in human relations, certainly since the Second World War.

THE GENUS OF COMMUNITY

The condition of modern human beings is quite curious when viewed from the perspective of other times. We are now all individuals. We have a notion of 'self' and can describe ourselves in terms of being 'unique'. I can list propensities and characteristics that I perceive to be more or less particular to me. Modern sociology, neurology, psychology and even anatomy seem to confirm this prognosis. I am me, you are you, she is her, he is him.

In an age of gender confusion and botoxic agelessness much more is up for grabs. To a certain and growing extent we can become who or what we want to be. We exist in what is a very self-centred universe wherein we are thought to construct ourselves (See Nemeth 2002 p. 6). This is comparatively new. The widespread use of the notion of community has been a post-World War Two phenomenon. But here we are, each one of us

B. Belton, Developing Critical Youth Work Theory: Building Professional Judgment in the Community Context, 01–13.

individualised human beings, seeking to express ourselves, while at the same time showing a desire to be part of greater wholes. We wish to 'commune' with others.

This anxiety not to be alone is a primal feeling close to other deep seated drives such as sex and eating. It is the force behind family and tribal affiliations epitomising the basis of our social psychological make up. It harks back to a time when the individual had no responsibility or identity outside the clan or settlement. One was of one's 'tribe' and later trade and that is what defined who one was. Later the notion of duty to God and a monarch kicked-in, but even then if a peasant was walking down some remote lane carrying a sword a knight riding by would be well within the bounds of justice to kill the peasant. To carry a sword was a prerogative of the knightly class; the only way the peasant could have got hold of a sword was to steal it from, and maybe kill, the rightful owner, another knight.

This was the fate of 'out-laws', banished from the protection of the law, the structure of order of the time. One was placed 'outside the law' not only because of the way one conducted oneself, but the how; your social category played as much of part in your condemnation as whatever it was you did to offend the ruling social elite.

The peasant with a sword would have represented anarchy and a threat to the feudal precepts of society which were based on everyone knowing their place and staying in it. From birth one was assigned to one's position in the social strata within a hierarchical society that had God and the King at the top and the peasant and eventually hell at the bottom. It was not possible to move around this order. One couldn't go to college and take a GCSE in 'Nobility' or an NVQ in 'Chivalry and knightly conduct'.

Mark Twain's novel, The Prince and the Pauper, first published in 1881, set in 1547, and tells the story of two boys identical in appearance – Tom Canty, a pauper who lived with his abusive father in Offal Court, London, and Edward VI, son of Henry VIII. The boys get to know one another, each becomes interested by the other's lifestyle, and fascinated by the fact that they have an uncanny resemblance. They switch clothes and lives temporarily. But a pauper cannot take the place of a prince. This would turn the world upside-down. This is what the English Revolution, the Civil War that pitted commoner Cromwell against King Charles I, was said to have done in the 17th century. Within the feudal order, relative to today, individuals had little responsibility. The section of society or order they were part of held their destiny within tight boundaries and this was seen as the Will of God or God's order. The King was seen as God's representative on earth just as the Pope was, and still is, seen to be descended from St Peter. The King was believed to be descended from King David. This faith continues to apply today as part of the justification for the British monarch being the head of State. The responsibility for a great deal of life therefore could be abrogated to the Will of God, the social order, the part of society that one was trapped within. This people trap is the archaeology and the genus of community.

The wish for community is an echo of a time much less complicated. Ours is an epoch where the individual fills up the space of thought. It was Freud who did much to open up this path laid by industrialisation and the coming of consumer society. We now account for everything as an individual. Our beliefs, taxes, system of justice, government and financial position are all premised on individual responsibility. Within the post-modern, post-industrial, capitalist world, the individual is the start and end of everything. The very basis of the capitalist system is the individual consumer buying things for themselves. But in the same way as our social evolution has outrun our biological evolution (standing upright has not helped our bowels, we have not really adapted to the modern stress of city living or curbed our animal aggression) our individualised state appears to be something we have yet to completely manage. The post-modern, individualistic existence has hit us so swiftly that we seem not to have had the time or the space to acclimatise. It seems that many of us do not feel emotionally secure with this state of being to the extent that we dig up all sorts of archaic attachments. This is perhaps most noticeable in the USA but it is becoming a western phenomenon. People seek out great, great grandparents in Ireland in order to be able to feel ok about marching in the St Patrick's Day parade. They return to Scotland to attend gatherings of clans that distant forebears were not slow to abandon given half the chance to get away from the tyranny of the Laird.

A typical 'born again' Scotsman showed me his family tree last year. His name was Grabolski. His grandmother's father, McCrimmon, was forced to leave Scotland and his family because the Laird had sold the tied farm that his ancestors had tilled for centuries, more or less condemning the family at least to destitution and maybe starvation. But McCrimmon had escaped via migration and met a woman in the US who was the daughter of a Native Canadian of Tatsanottine people and a French Carpenter named Lussier. Their daughter (Grabolski's grandmother) married a Jewish tailor from Poland whose son (Grabolski's father) married the daughter of a Jamaican couple, the mother being half Chinese and half black Jamaican. The father was the son of a poor 'red-leg' man of Irish decent and a woman who was the illegitimate daughter of an Italian naval engineer and a black sail maker from Kingston, Jamaica. Until Grabolski's lifetime the family had not been well off, living, since his grandparents' time, in the Lower East Side of

New York, below Delancey Street. Grabolski had made his fortune selling mats by mail-order. He was now, as an octogenarian, the honoured guest of the Laird. He paid thousands of dollars a year into his clan's finances that were mostly spent on the upkeep of the Laird's estates. For this he received an invite to the annual gathering, a newsletter three times a year and a bottle of clan 20 year, fine malt every New Year (Hogmanay).

This example provides some indication of how anxious we are to find affinity, a way of being with a group we can admire or gain the admiration of, or even just confirmation of our own existence as individuals who are connected to others 'like' ourselves. Finding confirmation of our own existence is perhaps a hard thing for the isolated, lonely individual in the sometimes harsh world we live in. We use football clubs, churches, community centres and many other ports in our storm of isolation to provide a sense of interpersonal 'coagulation' and/or psychic conglomeration in our lives.

THE CONCEPT OF COMMUNITY

The concept of community has caused what seems like endless debate with no real agreement about what it means or what it is. Over the years I have given this task to hundreds of students and the result has been little more than confusion. However, community continues generally to be accepted as a positive entity. It is a good thing, because it just is. It has warm and friendly associations of solidarity, commitment, mutuality and trust. It is something said to bring about closer, more harmonious bonds between people, or a place or situation wherein those bonds exist. Since some halcyon time, Western societies have apparently mourned for the loss of a 'spirit of community' although it is never quite clear what this spirit is. This is apparently a bad thing. Therefore, as the literature advises, professionals working with people should 'engage' with others in order to 'foster' their and our own 'sense of community'. This implies getting involved in building communities, community cohesion and community action to name but a few professional ambitions for community. These are the things one is advised to do though how we know when they have been accomplished remains at least an approximate vision. At what point do I recognise that a community has become cohesive? When might we be able to say a community action has been sufficient or completed?

From all the activity devoted to interpreting and/or acting out community, we can conclude that the idea or the hope of community is exceedingly important to contemporary society. The need or want to belong to a community has been portrayed as a central desire of what might be called post-modern humanity. A yearning for unity, safety and the sense of belonging certainly seems to be associated with community. But does this ideal community really exist outside the individual, social, academic or professional imagination? Is it anything more substantial than a conceptual metaphor? Why do we want to be some reshaped version of the Waltons or live in another Albert Square?

A DOUBLE-EDGED SWORD

Community as a notion is a double-edged sword. The stating of its existence implies a boundary, a division between people. It establishes those who are a part of it and those who are not a part of it. The defining of a community places some people within and other people outside of that community. The tighter the affiliation of any given community, the more impermeable its boundaries appear to be in terms of entry or exit, for example, the American Amish or North London Hassidic Jews.

People in a community have supposedly something in common with each other that distinguishes them in some way as different from members of other groups. The resulting labelling creates an 'inner' and an 'outer' – a them and us. The more binding the connections within a community tend to be, the more distinct is the division between those of the community and those alien to it. This makes the community a difficult place to leave for the threatening and relatively unknown outside, where the former community member will themselves be foreign. At the same time the interlocked community is almost impossible to get into, especially if one comes from a similarly comparatively impervious social situation. For example, it would be hard for someone born into a Hutterite community to leave that situation, and even more difficult for them to join, and be totally accepted by, a group of devout Zoroastrians. In this sense, while a community can be defined as a place inclusion it is also a means of exclusion – 'You are not like us, therefore you do not belong'.

We can see examples of this form of community exclusion from the international to the local arena. History is littered with groups being excluded from areas or countries to the end point of ethnic cleansing.

In order to be accepted by a community one must, to a greater or lesser extent, subsume oneself into the whole. Certain codes and ways of being that promote acceptability must be adopted and adhered to. Not to do so would mean becoming an outsider or being identified as a member of another community. In order to ensure continued connection, the community member needs to comply with the perceived needs of the community, which tend to override the need of any single member or minority of members, or their possible desire to dissent. A very 'solid' community will regard any departure from accepted norms as unacceptable. For instance, not wearing (or wearing) a particular hat at certain times or places, playing disapproved of music, eating 'unclean' food, looking at someone else in the 'wrong' way.

Is it not strange that we crave the sense of belonging we believe a community will bring at the same time as we are so 'individualised', demanding a notion of 'self'? We ask the question of who 'we are' and that this be both noted and celebrated. We insist that our 'personality' or 'persona' needs to be understood and catered for. We want to be distinct but also subsumed and the very last thing most of us want is to be totally and permanently alone but we also feel reticent about 'following the herd'.

LONELINESS AND THE BUZZ OF COMMUNITY

Loneliness is probably the most feared of diseases in the modern world. As a social condition it stands in contrast to the great desire of our times to be famous. Anonymity, the antithesis of being known, is the fearful fate of the early 21st Century. A person of no importance is the damned of contemporary society. 'Billy no mates' is the syndrome the likes of Facebook and Myspace exist to address (or sometimes confirm – a piece of cheese had 500 friends on Facebook at one point!)

The community seems to have the magical power to make the least of us more than we are. We can enter into a symbiotic (parasitical?) relationship with it. We can ride on its back as 'a part of'. We can disappear into the mass or hibernate in the conglomeration of individuals founded on dichotomy and yet still be 'somebody' – a member of a Scottish clan, the Ku-Klux-Klan, a Masonic lodge, a town called Dodge, a tribe, a vibe, a race, a place, a class, a caste, a culture, a Brazilian carnival salsa, a gender, a group of lads out on a bender, a political party, the same fly fishing club as J. R. Hartly, a rave, a Mexican wave, an ethnicity, a community.

For all of this we have to give up something to be part of a community. We are torn between our desires to be a unique 'I' and our need to be a 'we' and/or an 'us'. Is this why so few of us go to community centres or take an active part in the community? On the whole, the community does some pretty naff things – car boot sales (worse still 'table top' sales) and bingo spring to mind. There is of course 'Carnival', the appreciation of which even if you secretly hate it has become a Brownie badge for the 'funky middle-class' looking for a 'proletarian grove'. For all this, it is often much more of a 'buzz', especially for young people, to set up 'counter communities' that reject the values, rites, traditions and norms of the so-called community. But of course, there is nothing more conformist than mass non-conformity.

FREE MEN BREATHE CITY AIR

As we study community or 'engage with communities' it might be worth bearing the above in mind. Community is a phenomenon that is, in many ways, remote to our times. What is its place other than that it might make us feel good? If it just does this then why is it any better than soft drugs or booze? You might answer that it does an individual no harm and some people from tight or closed communities would agree with you. But others might see things differently. Those obliged to grow up in situations where relatively little knowledge permeates the walls of community have had to live with the often resulting pooling of ignorance that breeds prejudice towards outsiders. As this is going on, the community, keeping both distant and distinct, invites prejudice against it via stereotyping in the absence of any information coming out of the community to disprove the same.

An old Greek saying has it that 'free men breathe city air'. The anonymity of the metropolis, the escape from the prying eyes of the village or the tribe, was seen to be the most desirable way of living. It may be telling that it is often those who have never known the crushing nature that closely collective ways of living can promote who seem most avidly to seek to propagate community life, even though from Jonestown to Waco and the Heavens Gate cult, the whole idea has been shown to be tragically flawed.

Community has the ability to suffocate individual expression and openly persecute those who might seek to move away from the community's beliefs and norms. It is often the site of stereotyping, prejudice, discrimination and exclusion.

The whole notion of community is based on the idea of members complying with a particular, sometimes quite rigid, set of norms. To be outside those norms is likely to mean that one will be chastised or expelled from the community, usually to the distress of relatives and friends who might remain in the community. As such, the community rewards those who personify its norms and punishes those who do not reach its collective expectations. The community is authoritarian in this respect. It is reactionary, punitive, tyrannical and not interested in consensus. It is about the rule of the few by the many, the dictatorship of the majority, the creator and oppressor of minorities. It represses the wants and needs expressed by the minority to the whims and fancies of the majority.

OFFSIDE

In his film 'Offside', the Iranian director Jafar Panahi portrays a group of dedicated, rebellious and football-mad young women who want to attend a crucial World Cup qualifying match for Iran's national football team. The problem is that women are banned from the country's football grounds. To infiltrate the crowd the group are obliged to disguise themselves as young men. Panahi explained that the restrictions on women attending football matches only came after the Iranian revolution of 1979.

> *Because of this kind of ideology, the mentality of the people has changed, and so it is this 'official' mentality which is causing all the problems. But in my opinion, the majority of men do not have a problem with women attending matches. But since women were banned from attending, the whole atmosphere of the matches became very male and chauvinistic and rude, and it has by now developed its own momentum…Of course when you try to restrict something or implement a restriction it has to be based on some sort of law. But there is nothing in the law which has been approved by the Iranian parliament or anybody else which bans women from taking part. It has become a kind of unwritten law. The policemen and the soldiers too, have to follow these unwritten laws and they are answerable to their superiors for it.*

This is how many community norms come into being – as unwritten laws that impact on people's ways of being, thinking and action. Very often these norms go unchallenged because to challenge them means punishment or shunning. It is much easier to fade into the mass, to be a part of the relatively warm, seemingly friendly, conforming but harmonious throng. I just have to undermine my 'self' for the 'good' of the whole (as defined by elders, priests etc.) and all will be well.

But what of those people who do challenge or kick against the community's standards and expectations, those who rebel against either the codified or unwritten rules that dictate how they should behave - like the young women in 'Offside' and possibly like many of the young people we work with? What, at the end of the day, changes for the young women in Panahi's film or for any young person resisting their community's rules? Does rebelling against your community ultimately change anything? If it did it wouldn't be rebellion but revolution. To what extent does hegemonic thinking affect the way in which professionals engage with communities? And for what purpose are we engaging with these apparently well-chosen communities in which we work, which all seem to fit into particular social strata (we do not work with 'rich' communities – if such a thing exists)?

COMMUNITY AS CONTROL

Perhaps you might by now be getting a feeling for the primitive, carnivore nature of community and its reactionary and, at times, regressive use as a means of social control. Foucault's ideas relating to the individual demonstrate how people can be categorised and detached from the general social landscape as individuals being labelled as mad, criminal or young and so on. Foucault (1977) argues that this arises out of a need that contemporary society has to predict and control behaviour. Professionals, as agents of the State, look at someone, observe their behaviour and others who are thought to be like them. Records are then generated that enable us to make predictions about the future behaviour of those we have observed, which means effective control mechanisms can be put in place that will channel and/or deflect their activity into behaviour that we, our organizations, institutions and the State prescribe for them or approve of – community writ large.

Community can be seen as an idea that has evolved out of our society, a social system based on exploitation (that is what capitalism is) as another form of control. The more community controls, observes and corrects behaviour, the less there is for the State to do in this respect. The ambition for community in our society is for it to be used as a corrective instrument (as community police officers, community wardens and 'community watch' exemplify). That is why it is seen by many right-wing community enthusiasts, alongside the family, as having a responsibility in terms of social control.

Foucault would regard community as an aspect of the 'carceral' society and part of a general control process like prisons, schools or youth projects, which are all locations where 'specialists' are busy observing, recording, naming and predicting behaviour. The end of this process is the desire (albeit maybe sometimes driven by anxiety) to control. This might be for the best or the worst of reasons.

AN ALTERATIVE

Jürgen Habermas (born 1929) wrestled with these issues for many years. For him the means for us to be in association in a more positive way need to be premised on communicating in what he called a non-distorted way. While he does not devote himself to the question of community we can see that the least community requires from us is compromise. We need to distort our communication to the needs or requirements of the community. It is such forms of distortion which Habermas wishes to address.

For Habermas, the starting point in communication is not the need to look like or conform to the ways of others. He suggests that we do have an innate wish to communicate with others, sharing a mutual need to understand others through interaction. We are bound together by the process of understanding whether it is an agreement about 'what is' or a belief about the fundamental nature of existence. This could be seen as a kind of advanced survival mechanism. As such, anything that interferes with this need, the isolation of individuals or groups from as wide a plane of interaction as possible can be understood as damaging to everybody. So, for instance, single sex groups, forms of racial apartheid or the ghettoisation of people with disabilities, would be seen as not altogether useful by Jürgen the German.

The task Habermas sets us is to strive to understand others. In order to do this he does not ask us to highlight difference but seek similarity and promote forms of mutual participation in the experience of those to and from whom we wish to transmit or receive communication. This is what he calls intersubjectivity. From the start, the lines of communication are cleared of possible obstructions, such as perceived or actual difference, and the channels of potential understanding are opened.

The attempt to understand gives us an internal link with that which is external. My internal faculties are tuned to comprehend the person or group that is outside. At the same time, if all is going well, the person or group I am attempting to understand is also involved in the same task. This gives us a chance to become involved in, what Habermas calls, the 'life-world' of others and involve others in our life-world. The non-distorted communication is effected in the merger of life-worlds, the 'fusion of horizons'- no more 'outsiders' or 'insiders'.

Now this might all sound a bit new-age but it is quite a departure from our current way of doing things. A good deal of the work done with young people involves cutting down their horizons; zoning them off into discreet categories ('EETs', 'NEETs', disabled, Muslim etc) and limiting participation within gender, age group, ability, ethnicity, culture and so on. It does not, to any great extent, do what Habermas might suggest is the most expansive of activity i.e. formulate notions of what the life of others is like. Mary Wollstonecraft, in her 'A Vindication of the Rights of Women', makes a similar point with regard to the need for young women to communicate with their male counterparts.

Compared to notions of intersubjectivity, much work with young people is introspective or at least relatively limited in its breadth. Of course, there are reasons for this. The work may not be funded purely for the good of young people; the middle-aged, often white, often male, holders of the social purse, with no class or social affinity to the young people being worked on, may be inserting an element of control.

For Habermas, all situations (communities, cultures, traditions) are similar in terms of meaning. There is more commonality between say a group of white, working class, unemployed young people on a poor estate in Newcastle and a group of alienated Black youth in south London than there is dissimilarity. In order to communicate effectively it is probably necessary that this is understood. It is in the interest of the racist to point out overt and insurmountable racial differences. It is the tyrant's interest to divide and rule.

If culture is able to develop, if there is to be, as Habermas puts it, 'cultural and social reproduction', it is this coming together of life-worlds that will be promoted. The cutting off of life-worlds will cause the opposite reaction and lead to the stagnation and withering away of cultural and social environments. Our life-world interacts with and translates other life-worlds. They, at the same time, interact with and translate our life-world and a new life-world is born out of this expansive and expressive dialectic.

The project of intersubjectivity, through non-distorted communication, involves us in communication of rationally reached accord rather than the consensus of community, which is really a fait accompli implying that you are either 'in' or 'out' of step with the majority. Rational accord is essentially a social process that, unlike forms of community, enlarges collective and connective autonomy. It welcomes the character of the modern individual as a free, unaffiliated social actor, in that this extends the possibility of the discursive expression of another unique life-world, to enrich and be enriched. This offers the potential for an endless personal and group intellectual, social and spiritual growth by the interaction of the internal with the external.

The really difficult thing in all this is that it involves embracing our individual nature. It is not achievable by way of acquiescence to the assimilating bunch of human conformity that is the community, gender, nation or race. We have a need to accept our post-modern form - lonely individuals who, for all that, have the authority over themselves to become more, reach out, touch and enter into intersubjective relations with other individuals.

With the expansion and increased sophistication of electronic communications over the last few decades our potential to establish this intersubjective nexus has never been greater. Habermas begs us to accept and express our individualism to the utmost, to assert our autonomy and cease to abrogate our nature to the majority. For this we need the courage to see ourselves as separate, the strength and wisdom to deny the forces that would have us regress into self regulating and controlling tribal/community affiliations.

We are now potentially a planet of viewers. We are fascinated by looking at each other and ourselves. We are hooked on our uniqueness and our, often surprising, generality that paradoxically arises from the same. We, in our individuality, can derive freedom from the collectivity and the rejection of the mindless, slavish affiliation that community can't help being. That I am me and interdependent on the other 'I's (the generalized other) is a liberating notion. The 'I' is most threatened by the amorphous mob wherein exists 'treason' and intolerance of diversity. However, we have not been brought up to what Habermas proposes. We have learnt to want to merge with the whole, to disappear into the wallpaper. I would suggest that this is dangerous for that which is 'us' – the collective 'I'. The great tyrannies of Russia, China, and Germany were all based on the anonymous individual and the priority of the mass.

My hope is that we can make the most of what Habermas calls our 'cultural pre-understanding', our shared life-world, to create the 'communicative reproduction of society'. This seems a noble enterprise for the professional working with young people and it does not take too much imagination to see how the most straightforward activities can facilitate this adaptation of the inner to the social, to start to create a world made up of freely interacting 'I's, a ceaseless growth of life-worlds and the collective life-world.

So be wary of books and academics that wax lyrical about community. What is the reason for their enthusiasm – to whom does their message give power? I would counsel, nay implore you to behold the ambition for community with the greatest of scepticism. But equally I would ask you to hear this argument with cynical ears. I may be lying, joking, mistaken or simply mad. I may have been frightened by community when it snuck up behind me whistling the theme tune to EastEnders and never got over it. I offer you but one reality. However, Habermas offers us an alternative paradigm that can produce the effective communication of ideas in a world that often distorts efforts to communicate.

BIBLIOGRAPHY

Edgar, A. (2006). *Habermas: The key concepts*. Routledge.
Finlayson, J. G. (2005). *Habermas: A very short introduction*. Oxford: OUP.
Foucault, M. (1977). *Discipline and punish: Birth of the prison*. Viking.
Habermas, J. (1989). *The theory of communicative action* (Vol. 2). Polity Press.
Loewald, H. W. (1978). *Psychoanalysis and the history of the individual* (W. Hans (Ed.). Yale University Press.
Nemeth, D. J. (2002). *The Gypsy-American: An ethnogeographic study*. Edwin Mellen Press Ltd.

Skousen, M. (2007). *The big three in economics: Adam Smith, Karl Marx, and John Maynard Keynes.* M.E. Sharpe.

Twain, M. (2008). *The prince and the pauper.* Saddleback Educational Publishing, Inc.

Wollstonecraft, W. (2004). *A vindication of the rights of woman.* Penguin.

WEBSITES

http://www.religioustolerance.org/amish.htm

http://www.bbc.co.uk/london/content/articles/2004/08/11/communities_jewish_feature.shtml

http://www.hutterites.org/

http://video.google.com/videoplay?docid=3222765191601652959

http://www.guyana.org/features/jonestown.html

http://news.bbc.co.uk/1/hi/world/americas/431311.stm

http://www.trutv.com/library/crime/notorious_murders/mass/heavens_gate/1.html

COMMUNITY WORK IN THE UK – CONTEXT, ORIGINS AND DEVELOPMENTS

Community Development and Community Work in the Uk

The context of youth work is the community; for much of its history many of those involved in the profession have qualified as 'youth and community workers'. Today, youth workers will also be involved with, and qualified in, forms of community education, while youth and community work have long been in close proximity in terms of their professional genesis and political origin.

In this chapter I will look at the development of community work and discuss how the professional operating in the community, as we might be familiar with today, evolved as a profession with national recognition and a broadly acknowledged practice repertoire. This will provide a notion of the place and meaning of professional activity in the local social setting, which includes community education, community action, informal education and youth and community work. The practices associated with these disciplines have become set in the locale identified, cleared and claimed by and for community work. At the same time the tradition and purpose of community work has been translated into these related fields. This being the case, it is important for youth workers, educators and social workers to understand the development of community work because, as a widespread precursor of systematic community intervention, it has shaped the delivery and attitudes of professions following it historically into the local social system. This heritage is influential in terms of how youth workers, taking on the mantle of community educators, might understand the meaning and purpose of their role and the work they are tasked to undertake.

THE SIXTIES – THE BIRTH OF 'COMMUNITY WORK' AS WE KNOW IT

The 1960s saw the emergence of youth culture out of the post-Second World War social milieu. Identifiable groups of young people, by way of music, fashion, and in some cases political activity, began to assert values that seemed to contradict those held by the generation born between wars.

B. Belton, Developing Critical Youth Work Theory: Building Professional Judgment in the Community Context, 15–37.

It has been said that if you can remember the 1960s you weren't there. As a teenager in the middle of that decade I can say that there is some truth to this adage. Certainly for some it was a golden age but for others it was a decade that saw their scaffold of morality, authority and discipline collapse in a confusing and contradictory torrent of youth riot, protest, noisy electronic sounds and free love courtesy of what many saw as the indiscriminate use of birth control.

The growth of the civil rights movement in the USA, together with the rise of a discernable voice and presence of youth espousing a heady mixture of idealism, protest and rebellion, backed by a soundtrack of popular music based on Afro-American influences, promised an optimistic but less predictable future. This made for a strange fusion with the ethos of the Cold War and the seemingly imminent threat of nuclear oblivion. Compared to the drab post-wartime atmosphere of the 1950s, the following decade seemed like a brave new world wherein, in the words of Prime Minister Harold Macmillan (born in 1894) those in the UK had 'never had it so good'. While ringing true, juxtaposed with the possibility of Armageddon, it didn't convince everyone.

The publication of the Albemarle Report (1960) was something of a recognition of this great flux. However, while looking to restructure the outlook and response of youth work, the Albemarle Committee seemed in part to be motivated by a vague sense of threat posed by 'teenage consumption' – *a kind of selfishness which will not yield itself to any demand outside its own immediately felt needs* (1960: 33-34).

Music had become a form of international communication, inspiration and escape for young people. Change in how personal relationships were seen and what might be the appropriate context of sexual behaviour was motivated by a new boldness and candour in literature that infected television and theatre. The relaxation in censorship, the formation of the Feminist movement, fired by the myth of bra burning, alongside the concept of Gay liberation, gelled with affiliations to underground and counter-culture ideals proposing that new, deep and novel depths of spirituality and psyche could be plumbed.

While much of this atmosphere was quite dark, led partly by those influenced by the late 1950s social culturalist Beatniks, it was generated out of a faith that a better world was coming. Formally rigid social hierarchies, such as the notion that women were subordinate to men and children to parents, were becoming anachronistic and little more than the butt of jokes framed within the satire of David Frost (or more accurately his impersonations of his mentor Ned Sherrin). As a consequence, attitudes to sex were liberalised, racism for the first time was challenged, and the formally unquestioning respect for the authority of the family began to be scrutinised both publicly and privately. The formally relatively uncritical attitude to education, government, law, religion, and the concept of nation was weakening.

It is in this environment that community work first became politically and socially identifiable as an occupation separate from social work. And it was this 'sector' that became the host of youth work, its tool informal education.

As ideas about the role of the community worker in society arose out of ideals founded in government policy about the value of community leadership and participation, range of working methods and intervention techniques were developed. Community work, as a national phenomenon arose in this fluctuating social, political and cultural climate. It was made up of a range of initiatives and was to have an influence on the changing ideas of social and youth work. Some writers insist that the relatively isolated examples of endeavour in earlier times can be seen as a sort of primal precursor of the discipline. However, almost any group or local historical movement will have aspects that could be labelled community action. But it was in the swinging decade that the occupation of community work, as we recognise it today, began to take shape.

SOCIAL WORK PARENTHESIS

The primal roots of community work in Britain might be understood as part of the reform and radicalisation of social work. It developed as a method of social work rather than as a separate occupation. However, community work as a definite, emerging discipline in its own right had been proposed by Dame Eileen Younghusband in a report she wrote for the United Nations in 1959. In her book, *The Newest Profession: a brief history of social work*, she explains that community work had been previously practised in settlements and other settings, but that it only started to be more widely recognised as such in the last part of the 1960s. She states that it was used to help local groups to bring about desired change. Social surveys, social action, inter-agency co-operation and social planning were all aspects of community work.

These examples of developments in the decades after the Second World War show that new ideas, methods, attitudes and services were all struggling with old ways and attitudes but only really began to come to fruition in the 1960's. (Younghusband,1981; 28)

Younghusband developed ideas about the place of community work within social work, looking to a closer working relationship between professionals and their clients that might be of mutual benefit. In effect, this approach was understood to be able to contribute a variety of useful ways to enhance community development whilst enlarging the ambit of social work by obliging the profession to apply its knowledge and skills across this wider horizon. Cynically, this might be understood as a means of professional empire building while at the same time recruiting local populations to the greater cause of social betterment.

SEEBOHM: A STRATEGY FOR COMMUNITY

Community work was to be further elaborated and enlivened in 1968 by way of the Seebohm Report. This was a time when it became clear that social work theory and the organisation of social services were in need of significant development given the changing demographics of the modern welfare state. The reforms in social work, education, the youth service and in other areas such as health and planning had formally been seen to have absorbed community work. The emergence of the notion of 'people work' during the mid to late 1960s worked to push community work into becoming a profession in its own right. This process was energised by the desire of those taking up community work from social movements and political groups who saw the discipline as the means not just to achieve their specific political goals but also as a conduit to reform the conventional practices of these interest/pressure groups. Community work became a depository of all sorts of social agenda, a growing melange of purposeful reform that had more to do with the personal and political desires of practitioners and policy makers than members of any particular or general community.

The 1959 Younghusband report identified community work as one of social work's three methods being aimed at helping people within local communities to identify social needs and consider the most effective ways of meeting these needs. This foundation remained much the same over the following two decades. Younghusband noted that professional training in community work was almost nonexistent. This did much to provoke the development of professional training in Group Work and Community Organisation at the National Institute for Social Work Training. But it was nearly six years before community work became politically recognised as a strategy of social welfare. It was finally introduced into the State vernacular, perhaps tellingly, in a government draft white paper on the prevention of family breakdown and juvenile delinquency – a progression that as we shall see later may well have been related to the political and social upheaval in Britain at that time.

The introduction of community work as a separate discipline might be understood as part of the State's community strategy that looked to re-establish a credible relationship between the State and the working classes. Given the social, cultural and political changes taking place at the time, this relationship had been undermined while more conventional ways of nourishing the relationship (representative democracy for example) had become ineffective, subjected to waves of scepticism fuelled by the more liberal and growingly ubiquitous media. However, the development of community work was ostensibly based on humanitarian desires and social concerns which focused on improving relationships with and amongst the working class and other groups. These had become fractured as social and material improvements came about during the long post-war boom as the division between the poor and those advancing above the poverty line became more obvious.

For Younghusband (1981), economic and sociological studies of poverty demonstrated that large-scale change was required to tackle the structural causes of social inequality. But even if poverty and poor housing were eradicated, complex factors would continue to exist that contributed to social and personal distress:

In the whole period (of the 1960's) *knowledge grew about people who were delinquent, deprived, single parents, uprooted, homeless, grossly inadequate parents, alcoholic, addicted, handicapped; or suffering from acute or chronic or terminal illness or psychiatric disorder, or bad housing, chronic poverty, or destructive relationships, or social rejection, or other damaging experiences beyond their capacity to cope successfully. Naturally there were conflicting theories about contributory causation and appropriate interdisciplinary action, and the relative significance of personal and social factors* (p. 28-29).

The adoption of new community work methods and aims within social work was confirmed by the report of the Seebohm Committee in 1968. The resulting report pressed for a community-orientated family service. Other strategies such as social development areas, citizen participation, volun-tarism, social planning and the community development role of the area social services team were included. This all seems pretty familiar language to the contemporary professional ear.

Together with the urban aid programme announced in 1968, the Seebohm Report was the most important single event in the creation of the occupation of community work. Not only did it provide widespread publicity and legitimisation for community work within social work but in recommending the formation of a unified social services department it gave, in the last years of prosperity facilitated by relatively protracted economic boom of the time, the chance for an unparalleled growth in the numbers of community workers. It made a place for community work within the welfare state.

COMMUNITY WORK: PROGENY OF CONTRADICTION

It is important to recognise that community work, although partly recognisable as we would know it today, was, before Seebohm, orientated mainly around political campaigns rather than a professional occupation. The definition of community work tended to be tied to the particular issues of the day or to the agendas of the professional workers involved at any given time. Programmes of community groups were often built around the goals of the people who intervened to organise and, fairly straight-forwardly, help community groups. Thus in the 1960s community work was often defined in terms of the social and recreational needs of say residents in housing development areas. By the 1970s it had become identified with protest, conflict and campaigns around a number of inner-city issues. Later, the features of intervention remained relatively constant. Although the priorities of community groups and professional workers changed, they were often relatively ambiguous, partly because these constants, of which informal education was to become one, were not adequately defined in terms of purpose or method.

So the heritage and founding spirit of professional practice in the community context can be seen to have been set within forms of well meaning activism on the part of socially aware and/or politically conscious individuals and interest groups. However, the ladling of government policy, the means to implement State aims, over community work practice has predictably been a recipe for a culture of tension in the profession. The work has been practiced by those looking, with a variety of motivations, to defy or protect those at the nub end of society from the worst impositions of an exploitative State. However, these 'activists' took on the garb of a professional status that in practice recruited them to the cause of that very same State. The community worker from the 1960s became both an agent of the State and the enemy within. Phrases like 'working inside the system to change the system' rapidly became a mantra within the profession, although everything known about the nature of social environments indicates that individuals are more likely to adapt to contexts than radically change extensive and complex milieu.

THE DUAL DRIVERS OF DEVELOPMENT

The social, cultural and political changes of the 1960s, had much to do with defining nature of the work and the extension of its methods within social work. However, the initial movement towards community work can be split along two distinct lines.

Intellectual Radicalism/Bourgeois Guilt

A number of professional and academics groups, mainly those influenced by the political left, came together in the new universities and polytechnics that were part of the expansion of further and higher education in the 1960s. These groups were crucial in the generation of a number of new cultural and social issues. There was increased interest in alternative political structures and a fascination with the reification of the ideas of the 'left' as promoted by figures such as Che Guevara as well as Feminist and race movements such as Black Power. This was part of a search for alternative conventions to those that had been established during the post-war era. Ideas relating to 'change from within', 'evolution rather than revolution' as promoted by the Fabians began to gain credence.

At the same time the rise of counter-cultural ideas propagating alternative ways of being that demanded different values and expectations of society seemed to promote a more humanitarian form of social relations. These political and social ideologies informed and maintained veins of upper-middle class socialism (a historically strange amalgam of bourgeois guilt and the protracted adolescent rebellion of the 'chattering classes') that energised the development of the new professions. However, this was just one side of a social maelstrom out of which community work emerged.

State Agenda/Social Mechanics

The other side of what could be seen as the drive towards community work was the government ambition for economic recovery and social stability, two intimately related conditions in terms of the smooth running of capitalist social mechanics, which had been evident since the end of the Second World War, a period of relative social stasis.

Wartime rationing had ended and people were rebuilding their lives around changing family structures, a symptom of years of conflict and the concomitant expansion of industrialisation. Industry and businesses were rebuilt and by the 1960s an economic boom was blossoming, largely funded through the effects of American finance. It was a time of promises of a better world despite the shadow of the Cold War. The threat of nuclear holocaust to some extent brought people together under a common fear of Communism, stoked both by the government and the media. This also played a part in enhancing and strengthening the nation-state within the Western, non-Communist bloc. England's march to World Cup victory in 1966, symbolically over the footballing might of West Germany, was something of a peak point in this process.

The two sides of social, intellectual, cultural and political change, conspired together to create a feeling of solidarity in Britain at the beginning of the 1960s. In the changing environment their joint impact raised awareness about social and community work and the potential function of the forms of intervention that were becoming implicit in its practice.

SOCIAL DISAFFECTION/SOCIAL WORK INNOVATION

However, the early 1960s also gave rise to social disaffection and the emergence of poverty connected to the shortage of housing which grew to a chronic level. Family break-up and homelessness were increasingly becoming cultural and social issues. Social problems were recognized for the first time as moving beyond the personal to the public and social. As Younghusband (1981) put it,

> *To a considerable extent interests shifted from personal to social constituents of private sorrows and public issues as sociological studies demonstrated the effects of social attitudes and the environment on individual behaviour. These studies included social structure and institutions especially the class structure and marriage, family relationships and expectations and child-rearing practices, cultural patterns and values, social control and social conflict, social deviance, work and other roles, socialisation, social networks and social change.* (p. 29).

Britain had become an economically wealthier nation but the distribution of this prosperity was uneven. The situation of increasing poverty, social disaffection and housing difficulties appeared not to have been adequately addressed by the welfare state. With the rise of television and the mass media concerns about welfare, social work began to move from being mostly concerned with the personal arena to being involved with public issues. Mirroring this, the methods of work and intervention shifted from being focused on personal and childhood malaise (Freudian interpretations) to a concentration on the social and environmental causation of society's problems and personal difficulties.

Changes in the social structure and cultural understanding gave rise to developments in the methodology of social work as a response to the expectations and demands of a changing social demography. This included systematic assessment which was an attempt to identify the crucial aspects of a situation in order to target what, where and how to intervene. This might be thought of as the precursor of the common assessment framework.

Previously social work had been characterised in a comparatively shallow, often futile endeavour that lacked concrete aims and regular assessment. The new methods acknowledged the influential consequences that emotions might have on behaviour whilst recognising that providing for people's material needs could be a crucial aspect in meeting their social and emotional requirements. Anxieties around creating dependence were less to the fore. Two connected innovations were detailed case study records and supervision (duel and complimentary forms of surveillance and quality assurance). The objectives of community work were seen to be built on long-term contact and significant alterations in the client's lifestyle and outlook, both of which could be recorded and used as a means to establishing recognised and/or conventional practice. These aspects and characteristics of practice have endured into the present day as part and parcel of professional ambitions and strategies in the community context.

SOCIAL/PERSONAL PATHOLOGY

These innovations in the social work practice of the 1960s continue to influence the function of youth workers and social workers today. The assumption of social pathology that is evident in many of our justifications for intervention have their source in that time. Society is seen as being responsible for many of the problems individuals face and a communal or supportive response to problems is accepted as an effective strategy. However, the focus on individuals has become more intense. A young person can be seen as being involved in a double bind of social and psychological (personal) pathology. For example, one can be portrayed as lacking self-esteem because of poor parenting arising out of poverty and ignorance. Conversely, those accused of poor parenting can be seen as having a lack of self-esteem as a sort of interim causation. These opinions are cobbled together on the basis of both vague generalised criteria and sometimes an uninformed estimation of individual personality applied generically. However, they exist to justify intervention both at a personal and public level.

UPRISING AND THE CATEGORY OF 'YOUTH'

The 1960s was also a time of youth uprising both in the UK and abroad. The youth rebellions against tradition and the State were perhaps one of the strongest motivations for the rapid development of community and youth work, Young people at this time, began to protest about the nature of society on an international scale. This was the first time young people had been seen in a political light and this obviously posed a threat to the expectations of government. The notion of 'youth' as we know it today became an accepted political category rather than just a biological age group as it had been previously. They were given a social, cultural and political label and seen as needing to be treated as a category in their own right.

This rise of the category of youth was supplemented by a number of subcultures ranging from popular music to drugs, fashion, sex and religion. Rock stars moved from childhood rebellion figures like Elvis Presley (British incarnations included Cliff Richard, Joe Brown, Tommy Steele and Billy Fury) to propagators of revolutionary ideas through protest songs with singers like Bob Dylan, Joan Baez and Donovan. According to Wenborn (1989),

A revolution in fashion, music, literature and the arts took place as the opening up of mass communications helped create and sustain a world-wide youth market. Mini-skirts and caftans made it to the streets of London and San Francisco. The music of bands such as the Rolling Stones and The Doors came to symbolise their young audiences' rejection of parental values, while the 'pop art' of Andy Warhol and his bizarre entourage drew a cult following for its parodies of the images of mass-production. The word 'permissive' entered the vocabulary as sexual and social taboos were eroded by the contraceptive pill and the marijuana joint. (p. 342)

The rise of the flower-power movement, together with the pursuit of 'heightened consciousness', grew alongside the expansive recreational use of drugs and the international interest in Eastern meditation and oriental religions. While the vanguard of these collective phenomena were mainly upper middle/middle-class young people on both sides of the Atlantic, the search for a radical alternative to western culture dug deep into the younger population of Britain. However, the seminal working class incarnations of 1960s youth culture were the working class Mods and Rockers who, with a heady mix of heavy drinking, drugs and at times all out internecine war on the beaches of southern Britain, created a moral panic and genuine fear of youth. Made mobile by relatively high earnings with their Lambretta scooters (Mods) and motorbikes (Rockers) these youth tribes filled newspaper headlines and cinema newsreels with quite a different perspective of the young. Following hard on the heels of the Mods and Rockers in the gallery of intimidating youth were the more ill defined and barbarously rampaging football hooligans.

While youth had for decades shown the potential to present a threat to adult conventions (the Zoot-suited, Spiv-like pre-National Service age groups in the 1940s and the Teddy Boys in the 1950s) the young had never grabbed the level of political attention they commanded in the 1960s. What also needs to be remembered was that in the Mods and Rockers, for the first time, both genders were implicated. The black leather clad, Nihilistic Rocker females were the antithesis of the mini-skirted, white booted, pillioned, dolly bird Mods, but each were distinguished by an urge for liberation via the rejection of the norms of their relatively domesticated elders. The uprising of youth both against one another and against the conventions embodied in the State posed a threat to the social norms that had not been present in the past.

The youth phenomena grew to possess an international profile with mass student protests in Paris, the USA and Britain. Some of these were on a huge scale with powerful radical agenda. They often involved violent clashes with the police and in the USA and France paramilitary and National Guard interventions became a regular feature of such events. Student protests formed part of what some understood as a swing towards global, left-wing anarchist programmes. Movements like the Situationists in France, the first stirrings of Baader-Meinof in Germany, Black Power and the Black Panther Party in the United States, the Feminist movement in both Europe and the US seemed to confirm the breadth and character of youth.

An extract from The Situationist International in the early 1960's read as follows …

A new form of mental illness has swept the planet: banalisation. Everyone is hypnotised by work and by comfort: by the garbage disposal unit, by the lift, by the bathroom, by the washing machine. This state of affairs, born of a rebellion against the harshness of nature, has far overshot its goal – the liberation of man from material cares – and become a life-destroying obsession. Young people everywhere have been allowed to choose between love and a garbage disposal unit. Everywhere they have chosen the garbage disposal unit. A totally different spiritual attitude has become essential and it can only be brought into being by making our unconscious desires conscious, and by creating entirely new ones. And by a massive propaganda campaign to publicise these desires. (in Home(ed.), 1996; 4-5).

In Britain publications like School Kids Oz and the Little Red School Kids Book, which included sexual advice, information about the consumption of drugs, and how to organise protests and riots, played a part in politicising young people in a manner that seemed to many adults indecent. These publications coincided with a number of school riots in the 1960s. Perhaps one of the most publicised was the action at Islington Green School where students walked out and held a sit-down strike against homework, but uprisings were taking place all over Britain with different emphases and motivations. My own experience of school strikes were associated with coming out in support of adult trade union/industrial action or in sympathy with student protests against the Vietnam War, sometimes with the active support of teaching staff. Mr Jeffries (a geography teacher would you believe) took a group of us to the historic anti-war protest in 1968 centring on Grosvenor Square, home of the US ambassador to Britain. In 1975, following his example, I accompanied a group of young people I was working with to Red Lion Square to counter Fascist National Front protests against immigration. This demonstrates something of the political legacy created by young people in the 1960s.

As well as the youth uprisings which caused headaches for those supposedly in control, other social changes were taking place which created further complexities in Britain. Communal perspectives and ideas of self-enhancement created new expectations of social welfare services and community provision. The demand for equality of opportunity was first formulated during this period and could be understood to link directly to the changing perspectives on feminism, racial equality and co-operation highlighted throughout the 1960s in debates, riots and student protest.

SOCIAL TURMOIL

For all this, although many might have baulked at the suggestion or implementation of economic equality, the liberal perspective was energetically expressed in practice, arguing that everyone should have the opportunity to realise their potential and overcome barriers of health, economic considerations and other obstacles. This was the background to the push for the universalism of services and benefits.

The development of social welfare could be seen to add to the complicated network of relationships that made up the political and civil rights already established. The introduction of social rights and expectations into the welfare equation brought the individual and the community into a more intense relationship based on engagement in and control by the nation-state.

Housing

Housing in particular needed radical reformation. The 1960s saw growth in housing associations and owner-occupied housing. This was largely split along social class lines. Owner-occupation was depicted as being the better of the alternatives but the State had taken on the responsibility of providing accommodation for those who could not afford to buy houses. The aspirations of the New Town movement were to produce socially co-ordinated communities, but in the main State housing was understood as being mainly the resort of the working classes. This was effectively divisive and it played a part in the environmental causes of poverty, poor-health and crime. In caricature, the salaried middle-classes lived in owner-occupied suburbia; the waged working classes were accommodated on municipally rented urban estates.

Housing expenditure rose from £2.7 billion in 1960 to £7.3 billion in 1980. After 1954 there was a definite shift to resettlement and redevelopment located in the inner-cities, much of it of a high-rise nature. However, by the 1980s, this policy was largely regarded as flawed and much of this type of housing was demolished or refurbished by the 1990s. However, many of these over-spill or redevelopment sites were subsequently to become the location for inner- and outer-city social problems. Because of the impetus of the private market, and the presumed desire that everyone wanted to be home-owners, housing was never made the subject of a disciplined and socially cohesive programme. This situation was part of what fired the sub-prime disaster and subsequent recession of 2009.

Education

Education was also undergoing extensive changes with the introduction of new universities and colleges and an increasing agenda of equality of opportunity which did much to fire a restructuring of most of the country's educational services. Immigration became a political issue. The numbers of immigrants was to rise dramatically over the 30 years after 1950, fuelling the boom years of the 1960s. In the initial part of this period, demand for relatively cheap labour was the engine of immigration. However, as labour needs changed, limitations on immigration were called for. The age profile of immigrants was comparatively young relative to the rest of the UK at that time. This meant that the education and youth services were stretched more than say the health service.

Employment

Employment for most of Britain's new immigrant population tended to be poorly paid and concentrated in certain areas. It became increasingly evident that this created social disadvantage in employment, housing and education, perhaps inevitably sparking racial discrimination. The controversial Rivers of Blood speech by Enoch Powell (see http:// www.martinfrost.ws/ htmlfiles/ rivers_blood2.html) pre-empted and ignited major disturbances. The race riots in Notting Hill, and those in the United States, alongside the assassination of Martin Luther King, evoked more frustration and anger. These problems continued to be exasperated by insufficient adequate housing, rising levels of poverty, inequality and racism.

All this saw Britain enter a period of increasing turmoil during the 1960s. The UK was perhaps the most tumultuous State in the western world at that time. In France, for example, there were student riots that produced a disturbing level of violence but these were not coupled with the type of social problems that appeared to be inherent in British cities. In the USA there were race riots and the emergence of political movements emphasising the need for revolutionary change. However, although these were at least as violent as their European equivalents, they took place across the massive American nation with many areas simply immune from their impact. In the UK, because of a more condensed urban population, the concentration of poverty and inadequate housing was higher. Britain also had a highly agitated and politically educated class, led mainly by graduates from the new universities, who took on the ideas of Lenin, Sartre and Che Guevara. The social, cultural, political and intellectual position of Britain was, in the 1960s, the centre of a world social whirl.

Police, Social Control and the Mediation of State Violence

All this perhaps explains the birth of community work as an occupation in its own right, and the increased political agenda for the use of youth work as a vehicle for the re-creation of social responsibility and values of citizenship. It became clear that young people and the population as a whole could not be policed in conventional ways. These traditional, on the whole consensual, means of control relied on the agreement and support of those policed. At the same time, Britain in its politically democratic situation, proclaiming adherence to the spirit of liberty and the extension of freedom, could hardly be seen to bring in a National Guard or the military, as in the United States and France, in order to curb the violence of students and young people. However, at times, because of pressure on police resources, it was a close run thing.

Fighting on so many fronts, it was becoming impossible for the police alone to maintain order from the newly created housing estates, which had become havens of violence and drug use, to the coastal battles between Mods and Rockers. Add growing trade union and student unrest as well as the rise of the football hooligan, it was clear that there had to be some innovation in the realm of public order or private property would become so exposed that there would be no other option but to call in the troops. Not a few right-of-centre commentators had repeatedly demanded just this.

A re-interpretation of social control was needed if Britain was to avoid a form of social instability that appeared irrevocable with just the recourse to traditional methods of control. The rising threat of unpredictable ripples of both chaotic and revolutionary inclined violence threatened to undermine the whole environmental premise necessary to allow for capitalism to flourish. In addition, attempts in Ulster to curb civil disturbance and unrest through the use of the military had been shown as inherently flawed; using the naked force against mob violence appeared only to incite and nourish forms of organised resistance such as the UDA and the IRA. The State held a monopoly on the legal use of violence but the deployment of the same merely served to provoke an equal and counter response in Belfast.

Crime

With the social uprisings occurring on the continent and in the US it is not surprising that the political and social response to crime rose tremendously, even contributing to the enhanced perception of the need for increased numbers of community workers. The numbers of police officers rose from about 70,000 in the early 1950s to 107,000 in 1975. By this point over 14,000 staff were employed by the prison service with some 135 prison units to control and contain approximately 50,000 prisoners. This might be thought of as the start of the unprecedented growth in the UK's prison population that has grown unabated to the present day wherein record percentages of the British population are behind bars (outstripping any European counterpart). It is worth noting that this prison population is disproportionately black and young.

In 1962 there was a Royal Commission on the police as the approach of the force seemed insufficiently to challenge the growth in crime. This led to the 1964 Police Act which rationalised the system and clarified and strengthened police responsibility and authority. During this time the death penalty was abolished – temporarily in 1965 and permanently in 1968.

It can now be understood that the rise in crime during this period was caused by a complex mixture of social and cultural factors which were at the time hard to explain and even more difficult to change. Everyday life was, relative to the past, energized and volatile within a growing acquisitive ethos. The seeming collapse of respect for organised, communal, civic and domestic authority constituted a threat, particularly to those whose financial interests were dependent on the same.

The general instability resulted in a rise in police powers and more clarified civil responsibilities. These changes in policing were hastened by the increased professionalisation of the police force but overall this seems to have affected the social belief and trust in the police in a negative way. Some commentators state that it was during this time that the public's opinion of the police moved from consensus, dependent on communal consent and a helpful flow of information from the public, to military policing. This is seen to work in a suspicious way with little trust from the general public. The move towards our current 'surveillance society' had started.

Crime for the first time in modern history was highlighted on the political agenda. Violent crime was of particular concern, having risen by 5 or 6 percent during the 1930s and 1940s, it grew at an average of 11 percent annually after 1955. There were just under 6,000 reported crimes of violence in 1955 but over 21,000 in 1968. Little wonder that, in 1966, law and order for the first time became a major general election issue.

One response to the social uprisings of the 1960s was the advent of greater covert control together with encouragement for people to become more responsible citizens. People were also urged to use the system to make 'changes from within' rather than 'fighting against the system'. This is in line with Eric Midwinter's point that *Societies are moved to social amelioration projects under the duress of likely social fracture* (Midwinter,1994; 111).

At this time there appears again to be a strange connection between the professional, intellectual, politically motivated elite and the State in creating this alternative mechanism of social control.

The possibility of using community work as a profession in itself was initiated in the early 1960's by Dame Eileen Younghusband but was not taken on by the government until six years later, a point when conventional responses to the social uprisings had proven ineffective. The proposal for community work was set around a government agenda to curb the increasing break-up of families and the rise in juvenile delinquency. This was also tied in with the economic capacity to develop welfare provision. The number of people employed in health, education and welfare rose dramatically. In 1961 1.7 million people were employed in these areas, but by 1974 this had risen to nearly three million. The expansion of the welfare workforce was an economic measure which helped to maintain the principle of full-employment. Between 1960 and 1980 public expenditure rose by 100 percent with close to 70 percent of that increase being devoted to welfare programmes (Labour and Conservative administrations were both participants in this process). At present the National Health Service is the biggest single employer in Britain and the world's biggest employer after Indian rail and the Chinese Army, although both the latter workforces represent a far smaller proportion of the national populations.

LEGITIMATE CHANNELS

The role of the community worker was defined more clearly during this time. They were to work on housing estates with high crime, poor accommodation, poverty and a general lack of social motivation. Community workers were seen as co-ordinators and educators who could work with communities to use the tools of the State for change. Many of the initial models for community work were based on ideas about raising social and political awareness similar to the Freirian model of political education (an ideology that practically invites of corruption). Communities were encouraged to use legitimate, non-violent ways of working that encouraged the using of bureaucratic channels of communication rather than forms of protest (or riot). These could be seen to fit with the bourgeois systems and ways of working that were prevalent at that time.

The new methods of community work were also linked to a particular social ideology and the pathologising of people's problems which affected the methods that were chosen to intervene. In the first instance, caseworkers were inclined to focus on what might be broadly thought of as social pathology models rather than strengths. Their style was to be open-ended and non-directive. There was a propensity to overestimate the influence of the caseworker relationship and undervalue the impact of the social environment. In some extreme instances community workers claimed that social changes were their doing disregarding changes in housing or income for example.

In time this concentration altered again and what was understood as 'good' casework became whatever mode of practice seemed to be most effective in meeting the needs of clients. As such the demands on the caseworker grew and attention shifted from the emphasis on childhood experience to taking the current reality as a primal influence on conditions. Effort was placed on reinforcing the client's ability to manage and emphasis put on the strengths of existing and potential systems of support. The resulting methods of practice valued the self-awareness of the caseworker that was seen to improve their capacity to deliver an impartial service, untainted by personal preferences and dislikes. Later this was also seen to help preclude prejudices, culturally-based assumptions and values.

FROM INDIVIDUAL TO SOCIAL FOCUS (AND BACK AGAIN)

Within the social and cultural context, the move away from ideas of individualised living to more communal or co-operative ambitions had been another influence the changing motivations within social and community work in Britain. The social responsibility of the community worker shifting away from the individual to a more contextual, social response that sought social explanations for 'disaffection' or 'social ineptitude' on the part of the client had a political impact. Rather than problems being seen to be 'in' the individual as had previously been the focus of social intervention, community work took on, as part of its identity, the belief in community needs and responses, the causation of individual difficulties being seen to lie predominantly in the immediate social realm. Such situations were seen to increasingly demand a political response.

At the same time the focus within society at large moved from the individual to the community. It was perhaps inevitable that within community work that same alteration of focus took place. This affected the work undertaken and the very motives behind intervention in people's lives. The target ceased to be the individual and their personal history as the emphasis was put on the now and the individual as part of a social network. A more extensive range of techniques became available that were used in coordinated attempts to change individual experience by attending to their social context.

This broader perspective encompassed the influence of the family, neighbourhood, work or school relationships (negative and positive) and the ineffectiveness of attempting to alter isolated individuals. Consequently, the boundaries between casework, groupwork and community work became blurred as the goal was to use whatever methods and resources might be most effective in specific situations. A new emphasis was placed on the professional judgement of the individual practitioner. This was attractive to those who might have seen themselves as radical professionals as it offered a type of liberation from the constraints of State control. Over recent decades the room for professional judgement in the community context has been gradually curtailed by outcome orientations, targeted work, increased surveillance of client and practitioner alongside and part of assessment-led practice. This has been experienced as a clear reassertion of State control and the primacy of policy.

As the 1960s wore on, social change was encouraged, geared through consensus and partnership working with local government whilst encouraging community members to engage in legitimate political and social action for positive change. The phrase 'change from within' captures the ethos of the motivation of many community workers of this era and highlights the way in which the system was seen to be capable of meeting the needs of the people through the services it provided.

COMMUNITY WORK AS AN AGENT OF THE STATE

In effect the community worker became part of the means for the State to regain control. By involving directly or indirectly state-sponsored community workers based in both statutory and voluntary organisations, in the midst of the life of local communities and by encouraging local communities to use the systems of bureaucracy set within the local and national State, ambitions for potential change and feelings about social problems and unrest were able to be transmitted and exposed at an early stage. Ideas about action and change could be raised in public forums and community workers were made, albeit unintentionally, informers about that potential action for local government.

With local and national government involved in these processes, the ideal was that the needs of the community could be met through the relationships built with the community worker who was in fact playing a mediation role. Local government could then provide services or responses as it interpreted the needs of the community, or the necessity to dilute or placate potentially unruly groups. In other words, the local State had a way of subverting change or giving people something that looked like what they wanted when actually it was probably something that they didn't need. The community worker became the tool of amelioration and interpretation, involved in an intermediate process that refined dissension into forms of consensus, in effect strengthening the hand of the State.

By transferring and reciprocating the bureaucratic models and methods of working, such as the committee meeting, voting, agendas, formalising groups, and budget plans, social action within local community groups can be subject to limited forms of representational democracy. Examples such as youth parliaments abound. Community action can also be subjected to interpretation through further bureaucratic proceedings that inevitably find excuses for changes in plans. By using mechanisms approved by State control agents within communities that are looking for change, those same mechanisms are strengthened and thus enforce the sense of 'citizenship' and personal relationship to the State.

The energetic, raw disaffection of communities on the edge of change – which in the 1960s was seen as the potential fuel for revolution – is effectively processed through forms of bourgeois bureaucracy by the efforts of community workers. This is then interpreted as action by the State but actually serves to strengthen the State. The consequence of this is that communities become used to not getting what they want but instead receiving a State replica of what they wanted, or nothing at all. This leaves communities disappointed. It leaves them apathetic, unmotivated and potentially alienated from the decisions that are made about them. Consequently communities become apparently compliant and passive to State requirements.

An understanding of the context in which community work was established in Britain, the political and social motivations on which the establishment of community work was premised, demonstrates a clear political agenda underlying its development. It was so obviously related to the need to find alternative means of control to be allied to existing, more overt, means of State force.

So what has changed in respect to professional activity in the 'local social system'? Given the political, cultural and social environment we live in today, what justifications are given for professional incursions into the community? How have the methods of community infiltration and normalisation changed since the 1960s? Are we still as politically motivated or determined as workers or do we now have a general code of conduct that we are seen to adhere to? Do we still see society as essentially 'pathological' and its inherent problems being responsible for individual difficulties or have we moved away from this sociological understanding and towards characterising those we work with as being individually in deficit – lacking self-esteem, having attention deficits (ADHD) or conversely seeking attention?

CONCLUSION

The Younghusband, Albemarle and Seebohm Reports did much to inform each other in terms of techniques and purposes but they were all set within the social flux of British society from the late 1950s to the end of the 1960s and overall these seminal documents could not escape or fail to reflect the attendant fears, anxieties and hopes of the time. As such, the development of community work has shaped the delivery and attitudes of professions following it historically into the local social system and it is clear that the origin of British post-war State intervention into communities was premised on the perceived need to control sections of the population, youth being significant among these. This lineage has a definite impact on how community educators and youth workers might understand their role and purpose. Fear of the enemy within and the political instability this threatened at a time of perceived threat from without, together with the realisation that more direct or confrontational means of control were ineffective and impractical, provoked the development of more 'subtle' means of promoting social order; using social agents to champion the channelling of discontent and unrest into traditional, bourgeois, administrative, pseudo democratic procedures. At the same time these mediators, arising as many did out of the very culture they were in reality being employed to pacify, needed to believe that they were largely advocates of the people, acting as a vanguard for progressive movement.

It gradually became clear to communities and professionals that this was never the situation. This has led to apathy on one side and low morale on the other. However, many professionals working in communities, perhaps not totally conscious of the history of their role, maintain a level of activism under slogans like 'working within the system to change the system'. Sadly, with a few notable exceptions, megalithic systems tend to change (or dispense with the use of) 'rogue' individuals rather than the other way round. At the same time, bold speeches at youth and community work conferences which basically prescribe the tearing up of job descriptions and/or leaving employment if it fails to live up to radical interpretations of community activism, dissipate as ineffectual and silly idealistic hot air. The adage that there is nothing more conformist than mass non-conformity again rings true when the self-acclaimed rebel, having alerted those they rebel against of their position, witness their dissent being digested into policy and as such ameliorated to the cause of the system.

In Britain community work practice, which now encompasses and is implicated by youth work and the role of the same in community education, is situated within the historical and social context of a society whose political, legislative and educational institutions grew out of and confirmed the values, aims and growth of Empire, colonialism and slavery. Even a glimpse at the post-Second World War period confirms that the influence of these comparatively historically recent global and social phenomena, which energised and prepared the ground for modern monopoly capitalism, have never really gone away. Their effects and legacy cannot be ignored, although in much of the literature relating to youth work and informal education they are.

The background to our work has been culturally shaped by the colonial era which has only in the last century reverted from naked physical 'engagement' to (mostly) forms of economic and professionally mediated colonialism. Like other considerations, these historical foundations have an impact on the contemporary social situation.

The above history of community work demonstrates that State action is taken not to primarily better any given group but to control populations to follow its own capitalist (exploitative) logic. It achieves this partly by corralling them into mostly competing and/or inter-threatening categories. Youth is one such.

This chapter asks the reader if the ambitions of social agents to work at ('incline') the 'shaping' and 'changing' of young people ('natives'), to 'acclimatise' them to particular interpretations of 'democracy' and 'citizenship' smack of the aspirations of colonial society?

The idea that professionals 'empower' assumes their clients are relatively 'powerless' compared to the 'professional giver of power'. The logic of any project to 'enable' is based on a deficit model, albeit not totally conscious on the part of any particular individual, which sees certain groups as relatively 'dis-abled'. Work founded on such assumptions, which are reminiscent of the basic premise of the well-meaning missionaries of bygone centuries, seems to beg reassessment. (They were at the same time also part of the justification for colonialism). It is hoped the analysis in this chapter will be beneficial in this respect.

Why do we, as supposed 'community educators' assume a particular community needs educating? Is it ignorant in some way, if so, how is this established? Who decides what facet of education to deliver? Should 'professionals' seek to 'change' and 'educate' a community when most of the people in the 'targeted' community have not asked to be changed or educated? Do professional ambitions for communities demand at least a bit more analysis? Does the 'professional' voyaging boldly, although uninvited, into the 'community' have echoes of the, albeit well meaning, missionary sallying forth to bring 'civilisation' and 'salvation' to the 'natives' of distant lands (see Fanon, *Black Skin White Masks* and/or *The Wretched of the Earth*)?

The informal educator in the community, looking to promote 'learning' is directly or indirectly sponsored by a State which does not have 'helping' or 'supporting' others as its intent. As professionals we are historically part of a political strategy designed to achieve outcomes that are at least in part set in the macro-economic realm. How can we work 'effectively' unless we have theory that allows us to take this into account? Do many writers on community education (debatably themselves products of and adherents to the 'deficit' models indicative of 'colonial society') have the capacity to help us decipher and work within this milieu? If not, why are we directed to them and others with equally ill-equipped consciousness (see Carmichael and Hamilton's *On Black Power*)?

If something is bad, or flawed, or dangerous, it is enough if we expose it for what it is – Geoffrey Mason

BIBLIOGRAPHY

Carmichel, S., & Hamilton, C. V. (1967). *Black power*. Vintage.

Fanon, F. (1967). *Black skin, white masks*. Grove Press.

Fanon, F. (1965). *The wretched of the earth*. MacGibbon & Kee.

Marwick, A. (1998). *The sixties – cultural revolution in Britain, France, Italy and the United States*. OUP.

Midwinter, E. (1994). *The development of social welfare in Britain*. OUP.

Thomas, D. N. (1983). *The making of community work*. George Allen & Unwin Publishers Ltd.

Wenborn, N. (Ed.). (1989). *The 20th century – A pictorial history*. The Hamlyn Publishing Group Ltd.

Younghusband, E. (1981). *The newest profession – A short history of social work*. Surrey: IPC Business Press Ltd.

THE EXPERIENCE OF COMMUNITY

Never be limited by other people's limited imaginations...If you adopt their attitudes, then the possibility won't exist because you'll have already shut it out ... You can hear other people's wisdom, but you've got to re-evaluate the world for yourself... Don't let anyone rob you of your imagination, your creativity, or your curiosity. It's your place in the world; it's your life. Go on and do all you can with it, and make it the life you want to live...
–Dr Mae Carol Jemison *Finding Where the Wind Goes: Moments from My Life*

The role of youth workers as community educators demands interrogation. If we are to educate a community we must first identify it. Why and how do we 'label' an estate, a neighbourhood, a racial or religious group as a community? Once the label has been adopted it acts as a means of inclusion and keeps others out. It does not take much imagination to see the dangers of how prejudice might play a part in 'enhancing community cohesion'.

Of course, what is seen as positive right now may not last throughout history. Today, I might not be in much danger identifying myself as part of the 'Gypsy community'. Indeed, there might be some benefits but it was a relatively few years ago when that identity would warrant transportation to a death camp in some places. This was part of the consequences of what Ashley Montagu has called 'Man's Most Dangerous Myth'. Do we need to be careful when playing our parts in 'generating communities'?

The word 'community' is used in a variety of contrasting ways, often rhetorically or based on sentiment; general and ephemeral ideas like 'spirit' and 'ethos' are deployed to explain the notion, but in practice do little more than make an ambiguous concept more vague. We might attempt to clarify what we mean when we use the word 'community' and look at how community can be approached as a symbolic construction but can community be seen as an expression of the 'generalised other', or is it more than this?

This chapter is about understanding the nature of community. There are endless definitions of what constitutes a community. People have written

B. Belton, *Developing Critical Youth Work Theory: Building Professional Judgment in the Community Context, 39–54.*

about the subject for many years as if it were a definite entity like an enduring landmark, a sea or a mountain. But the notion is comparatively new, say compared to words like 'family' or 'village' and it has changed its meaning over time. It is hard to find in popular films, newsreels or plays before the 1960s for instance.

THE 'ASIAN COMMUNITY'

Ideas about the existence of 'the Black community' or the 'Asian community' for example have proliferated but there is no clear sense of what these collectives might realistically represent. Who comprises the 'Asian community'? Indians, Pakistanis, Bengalis, North Koreans, Japanese, Australians? Are all or some of these more national groups than communities? What does one have to do or be to qualify as a member of the Asian community? Perhaps the reference to the 'Asian community' is just a way of pointing out the local 'brown people' without actually stating as much. The fact is that it would be hard to identify the Asian community or any specific Asian culture. For example, over 150 million people live in Bangladesh, about a quarter live in urban environments and approximately 30 million of them are not Muslim. The country is 144,000 sq km in size – more than ten percent bigger than England. About 0.5 percent of the British population in 2001 described themselves as 'Bangladeshi' (about 0.3 million people) although there may be a significant group of people with Bangladeshi heritage who identify themselves primarily as British. Bangladesh voted Khaleda Zia their first female Prime Minister in 1991. She would be elected to power again in 1996 and 2001. Another woman Prime Minister, Sheikh Hasina Wazed served up to 2001. There are close to 40 language groups in Bangladesh (about 14 million people speak Chittagonian for example). The most popular sports are cricket including ten women's teams in a national league and football but the country is a huge producer of baseball clothing. Bangladeshi women compete in most sports and have won medals in international swimming, shooting and martial arts events.

This represents a massive cultural diversity which includes food, dress, customs, traditions, literature, music, family and gender relations. What constitutes the 'Bangladeshi community' say in Norwich? I have worked with Bangladeshi groups in East London on and off for close to 30 years. I suppose East London Bangladeshis would be described as a fairly tight community although I'm not sure they are any 'tighter' than say East London Lesbians – how would you measure that comparison? I was recently told by an experienced youth work colleague that East London Bangladeshis 'are all Muslims' and that they 'do not take an active role in the community' as the are 'not allowed out'. Bangladeshis have been in East London for a long time. A fair number of people who might describe themselves as East London Bangladeshis have married people with origins in India, Pakistan, Somalia, Britain and numerous other places. Their children have various affiliations and identities and like many young East London Bangladeshis some are drawn to reformations of Black British culture. Unlike my colleague many East London Bangladeshis have lived and worked in other parts of the UK, Asia, America, Africa, the Middle East and Europe.

I would argue that you might find it hard to find a typical East London Bangladeshi in terms of belief, gender attitude or any number of criteria. I would venture to say that East London Bangladeshis are like most other East Londoners – pretty much a difficult bunch to pin down with regard to identity and affinities. Even with three decades of professional experience, working with East London Bangladeshi young people and youth workers and being a life long resident of East London I can't even say if most East London Bangladeshis support West Ham United let alone what the general attitude to female 'participation in the community might be'. This said I have known some powerful and forceful East London Bangladeshi women, some of whom would not be too happy about a professional making very general statements about them and their 'role in the community'.

Going just one step further, the Indian sub-continent alone is home to a far wider range of cultures, religions, dialects and languages than might be found in Bangladesh. For example, China has about 50 million languages and dialects. For someone in London to say that they are 'working with the Asian community', is, in reality over ambitious and perhaps a little thoughtless.

COMMUNITY FEELING

In a sense, therefore, community might not be a thing, a certain collection of people or any particular place. Community is perhaps more constructively thought of as a feeling or a sentiment that is captured in events or constructions and it is this that we will be exploring during this chapter.

What do you think community is? It is likely that your idea of what it might be is going, at least, to be slightly different from what I might believe it to be. Some might claim that their community has helped them understand who they are but that in itself is a rather vague notion – who am I? The answer to that question changes over time and place. Who I am today is not necessarily who I might be in three years time or who I was 15 years ago. Brian was different when he was 13 to what he is at 54. At 13 I thought I couldn't care less at 54 I know I do care a lot. That alone makes a world of difference. Although we might argue that aspects of who I am have remained the same, the aspects one might name as non-changing today might be quite different from those we identify on our 79th birthday.

Over the last thirty years, television has seen a proliferation of depictions of community. *Coronation Street* and *EastEnders* are perhaps the most enduring examples but one of the most thorough is *The Simpsons*. It includes the school, workplace, leisure activities, neighbourhood relations and family interactions. Springfield, the home of the Simpson family, is in no particular place in the United States and it exemplifies the homogeneity of expectations contained within the notion of community (warts and all). Would Bart benefit from informal education? Might Homer or any or all of the population of Springfield be able to capitalise on the provision of community education? Bart doesn't grow up but does Homer? *The Archers* on BBC Radio Four is another popular creation based on 'community experience'. Is Ambridge like Springfield? Might what is good, in terms of 'learning provision', in Springfield necessarily work in Ambridge or Walford or Weatherfield or with Bangladeshi East Londoners? Are the tactics and philosophy of community or informal education transferable from place to place and from culture to culture over time?

IN THE COMMUNITY

From my earliest days, my family travelled from our East London home to the hop-fields of Kent where I played and worked with a strange and intriguing assortment of Gypsy and *Gorgio* (non-Gypsy) children. On my sixteenth birthday, I stood on a pub table at Horsemonsden horse-fair – a regular family event – and sang *I'm a True Didikois* to the applause of what I considered 'my people'. As a teenager I attended and was repelled by cock and dog fights. I witnessed bare-knuckle boxing, both organised and impromptu. I experienced this 'sport' at close range in a gravel pit in Essex. I fought one Ryan O'Connell in front of a crowd of Irish Travellers and English Gypsies losing a purse of £50 a torturous hour later. I have rubbed shoulders with Gypsies and Travellers from Essex to Hungary and the south eastern United States. I have practiced as a professional youth and community worker with Gypsy families on and off sites. I have served on a national organisation concerned with Gypsy education and have written, lectured, spoken, and argued about Gypsy issues from Canning Town to the South Atlantic, from Shanghai to Lusaka.

What I have from all this are essentially stories – knowledge of how they are made, their social force and what they collectively create. People and what their stories can tell us about the world and 'reality' have been contorted to become 'theories' of community and disguised as the truth but this too informs us about the character of society. However, there are many good stories and thankfully not everyone has theories to peddle.

I was brought up with the idea that I was 'different', that others were quite separate from my family. It was never said that 'we are Gypsies' or 'they are 'Gaje' (non-Gypsies) but it was understood that 'we' were not like 'them' and 'they' were not the same as 'us'. We did things that 'they' didn't and, in truth, we handled this by developing an attitude that 'we' were 'better' than 'them'. There was no straightforward explanation for this conclusion. Who we were served as enough clarification and what we were was 'us'. But this exclusivity was not a race nor was it an ethnic type. Those who were not 'us' saw us, depending on the context of their view of us, among other things, as 'costermongers', 'robbers', 'con-artists', 'mumpers' and 'Gypos'. So, it is perhaps not surprising that from a young age I was interested, although truly unconcerned, in the reasons for how we were perceived and defined. It seemed certain that how I was seen had something to do with the way my family lived and what we did for work. Our income and how we got it was an aspect of this and from the age of five, I personally earned money within the family business and had an extraordinary level of disposable income which set me apart. However, this, for me, was simply part of life. The work I did and the money I made was a facet of my family life which itself was connected to a wider set of values presided over and dictated by my paternal grandmother.

For all my compliance and acceptance with these seeming norms, they were, for others, processes that they seemed unable to comprehend from my perspective. My family's waves of income oscillated with the seasons, according to our 'portfolio' of self-employed activity. We had a propensity to acquire the outward trappings of wealth- clothes, jewellery, motor vehicles. My brother and myself, acquired the latest and most expensive toys that, unbeknown to our envious childhood peers, were in fact being used by us in transit between being bought and sold. I learnt never to love a toy too much as such things were always in a state of coming and going. Retrospectively, it seems to me that the way my family made a living caused us to be summed up on a continuum that moved from untrustworthy to mysterious and led to responses that started at suspicion and sometimes developed into superstition, fear and hate. Although, unseen, there were times when we lived a relatively impoverished existence, in damp and freezing conditions in the winter, fighting serial bankruptcy and spending inordinate amounts of time stretching the family food budget with manically judicious shopping habits.

My family way of life and the attitude of the wider community toward us turned us in on ourselves. Not trusted, we trusted no one but each other.

This caused 'our' way of doing and seeing things to become increasingly ingrained. We became even more 'us' as outside influences grew more remote, aggressive and foreign, until every encounter with the wider world could be interpreted as a reaction to 'us', which in the process further confirmed that 'we' were different to 'them'. A two-sided reaction.

Life became a struggle of us against them. Fidelity and loyalty to each other was our credo and what we put our faith in. The godhead was my grandmother. For instance, when I was subjected to bullying at school, it would be inevitable that my family would become involved in 'setting matters straight'. Any oppressor would be held down while I was obliged to give them as good as they had given me. Refusal on my part would be met by threats towards me from my family (evoked by my grandmother). This of course led to my brother and myself being subjected to a strange hybrid of respect and resentment that in turn caused a mutual identification and sympathy between ourselves and others who experienced alienation.

As a boy my attraction towards what some might understand as Gypsy 'cultural pursuits' or 'customs' was very powerful. While many of my school-age peers were hanging around street corners and others played table tennis as the 'soul vultures' did their best to 'win them for Jesus' at the local church youth club, my Gypsy contacts introduced me to stalking pheasant. They took me into the brutal, fearsome yet exciting worlds of coursing, dog and cock fighting. With them I built my own scrambling motorbikes and raced them. We brewed and consumed various forms of near life-threatening hooch. I was exposed to a vibrant and fascinating world of gaming, bareback horse riding, poaching, gambling, singing and money-making trading. This interaction took me to bare-knuckle fighting events and catapulted me to the centre of that violent yet adrenaline-intoxicated universe. I found that this dimension was not populated by 'ethnically pure' Gypsies, or any particular type of person. Each venue was a meeting of worlds – class, culture and status meant little if anything. One owner of a fighting cockerel was a middle-aged Trinidadian, a Chinese/Bethnal Green (another of London's East End villages) teenage girl owned and trained the most astute poaching lurcher I have ever seen. For an energetic, restless, imaginative and intelligent young person, this cosmos of melding offered much more than the norm. As memory, my 'Gypsy-boy days' are a psychic-rainbow, firework show that informs and enriches every aspect and moment of my life.

My brother became a police cadet while I gravitated towards the milieu of 1970s English youth violence and rebellion. As one of West Ham United's 'Gypo' cohort, a fearsome spearhead of the Mile End Mob, I sallied forth in the football wars of the urban waste lands of the last quarter of the twentieth century while mixing socially with the array of migrant communities that populated the East End of London at that time. My music was Black and my clothes were Rude Boy ominous, mirroring the garments of the young Caribbean Buffalo Soldiers that fought on arrival. The business life I pursued with my family saw me 'Dancing with Jews' and I became a favoured 'rogue trader' of Indian wholesalers. All the time I became more the 'other' and less a product of the norm.

This life caused me to begin to read. Initially this was related to football, horses, dogs and motorcycles but then I picked up books on poker which led me to psychology and biography. I was a Gypsy by blood, culture, and tradition but the way was paved to literature and a subsequent curiosity about classical music and theatre. In the same way I made myself fist-fight using bare and bloodied knuckles and matched myself on two mad wheels, flying at 'a ton' over Bow Flyover, I forced myself to listen to vinyl Bach and Beethoven at Canning Town library until my mind became attuned and addicted. I used the money I accrued to buy concert and theatre tickets. I saw few lone working class boys at the Royal Festival Hall or the National Theatre but I made new friends – Arthur Miller, Harold Pinter, Steven Berkoff, Tchaikovsky and Vivaldi, who seemed to understand my condition, my frantic feelings. The caravans of my Gypsy mind were moving. I was travelling! An alternative route might have been a respectable yet impoverished apprenticeship, an early marriage or the hell of being locked into the domestic incarceration and the chains of a mortgage that would tether me to a few square yards of sterile earth for a third of a century of toil, untidy affairs, anxiety, care, illness, stress and a pension of divorce and clinical depression. But all that never happened. Instead I travelled. *That's why I'm a True Didikois.*

This was my experience of how the process of being a Gypsy – an identity, part of a collective and connected social entity – worked. It was a machine of perpetual motion that was fed from the outside and, at the same time, was energized from within. My definition of myself interacted with confirmations from the 'other' to make who I was. However, when, in later life, I began to explore the nature of race and ethnicity it became clear that these notions are quite fragile and vague concepts and I was confirmed in my view that they are socially generated. I recognized that something of the affinity I believed in, that I had a faith that I was part of, did not exist in any concrete sense. As I looked at groups and populations of Gypsies, Travellers, Van Dwellers and Roma, I discovered that each group had a tremendously rich and diverse heritage and history and that there was very little of any significance that one might say for definite about what these groups or even those within each group had in common. What I had thought my community told me about myself had seemingly all been little more than at best legend and at worst illusion.

HIBAKUSHA

Geoffrey Wansell is an author and free-lance journalist who now works principally for the Daily Mail and the Daily Telegraph. He recently wrote the following piece for the Daily Mail, printed March 30, 2009. Like a good deal of Geoffrey's work it demonstrates the connection between individual, family, local, national, international and historical experience and perhaps the impossibility of confining any particular focus to a community perspective. I thank him for his permission to use his work to illustrate these connections.

Quite simply, Tsutomu Yamaguichi, is one of the luckiest men in the world.

This slight 93-year-old man with white hair, who is now largely confined to a wheelchair, was formally recognised this week as one of the tiny handful of people to have survived not one but both of the American atomic bombs dropped on the Japanese cities of Hiroshima and Nagasaki in August 1945 – effectively bringing an end to the Second World War.

Known in Japan as the hibakusha – literally 'the explosion affected people – Mr Yamaguchi had long been recognised as a survivor of the nuclear explosion in his home town of Nagasaki but on Monday officials there certified that he'd also survived the Hiroshima blast three days earlier – where he'd suffered severe burns to his upper body and temporary blindness.

But for years, the dignified, unassuming Mr Yamaguchi has made light of his terrifying ordeal on those August mornings six decades ago when the original weapons of mass destruction were released on the unprepared, predominantly civilian populations of those two cities in southern Japan.

Rather than campaign, or complain – even though he spent 16 years wrapped in bandages to help him recover from severe burns – this former draughtsman and engineer rarely talked about what happened to him.

But now, dying of cancer, a disease that struck down so many of the other innocent victims of the blasts, he has decided to speak out.

'After I die I want the next generation hibakusha and the children after that to know what happened to us', he insisted this week, convinced that the use of atomic weapons should be abandoned forever.

Mr Yamaguchi is quite right. No one should be allowed to forget the devastation caused by those two atomic bombs – the only ones ever to have been used in warfare. An estimated 140,000 were killed on the first morning in Hiroshima, and a further 70,000 died within 24 hours in Nagasaki.

Nor should the world forget the dreadful tragedy that it brought into the lives of every person who survived the deadly blasts, which saw hundreds of thousands more die in the years after the explosions from illnesses, and particularly cancer, brought on by their exposure to radiation.

Mr Yamaguchi certainly knows that. His only son Katsutoshi and his daughter Naoko were ill for much of their lives as a result of the exposure to radiation, while his son died of cancer in 2005 aged 59. His wife died last year, at 88, from kidney and liver cancer.

That was the terrible price those ordinary civilian victims paid for American President Harry S Truman's executive order to launch nuclear attacks on Japan without warning in the summer of 1945 in an effort to bring a speedy resolution to the War.

It is a decision that angers Mr Yamaguchi to this day. He accepts it's 'a miracle' that he survived both bombs, but says: '...having been granted that miracle it is my responsibility to pass on the truth to the people of the world'.

The truth in his case is truly horrifying. But to grasp the extent of his nightmare, and his good fortune, we need to travel back in time to that summer six decades ago when the sky first turned black, darkened by the mushroom cloud of an atomic bomb.

At the time Mr Yamaguchi was a 29-year-old technical draughtsman designing oil tankers for Mitsubishi Heavy Industries in his native Nagasaki. He was a family man, and his first child, son Katsutoshi, had been born that February.

In May 1945, with Japan struggling to keep its fleet of oil tankers afloat in the face of attacks from allied submarines in the Pacific, he – together with two work colleagues, Akira Iwanaga and Kuniyoshi Sato, were told to go and work on a new project in Hiroshima, 180 miles away to the North East.

47

But by the beginning of August the task was completed and the three men were ordered back to Nagasaki. It was then that fate took a hand.

Early in the morning of Monday August 6, the three left the company's dormitory and set off for the Hiroshima railway station and the trip home. On the way, however, Mr Yamaguchi realised that he had forgotten his personal name stamp and jumped off the bus to go back and collect it, while his two colleagues went on ahead.

Mr Yamaguchi hurried back, picked up the stamp, jumped back on the bus and got off at the last stop to begin the thirty minute walk to the Mitsubishi Shipyard. It was shortly before 8.15 in the morning.

'It was very clear, a really fine day, nothing unusual about it at all' he recalled 60 years later. 'As I was walking along I heard the sound of a plane, just one. I looked up into the sky and saw the B-29, and it dropped two parachutes. I was looking up into the sky at them, and suddenly ... it was like a flash of magnesium, a great flash in the sky, and I was blown over'.

The American bomber Enola Gay, named after pilot Colonel Paul Tibbets' mother, had dropped a 13 kiloton uranium atomic bomb, nicknamed 'Little Boy'. It exploded with devastating force 580 metres above the city. Mr Yamaguchi was barely 2 miles from the epicentre of the explosion.

'I didn't know what had happened,' he remembered later. 'I think I fainted for a while. When I opened my eyes, everything was dark, and I couldn't see much. I thought I might have died, but eventually the darkness cleared and I realised I was alive'.

'When the noise and the blast had subsided I saw a huge mushroom-shaped pillar of fire rising up high into the sky. It was like a tornado, although it didn't move' he said. 'The first thing I did was to check that I still had my legs and whether I could move them. I thought, "If I stay here, I'll die"'.

'Two hundred yards ahead, there was a dugout bomb shelter, and when I climbed in there were two young students already sitting there. They said, 'You've been badly cut, you're seriously injured.' And it was then I realised I had a bad burn on half my face, and that my arms were burned'.

After spending two hours in the shelter, the injured but still determined Mr Yamaguchi set out for the shipyard, picking his way through a wasteland of devastation – to discover that Mr Iwanaga and Mr Sato had also miraculously survived the blast.

Unsure about what to do, they decided to return to their dormitory on the other side of the city. As they picked their way through the ruins the true horror of what had happened was all around them – countless bodies, shattered buildings, and, above all, children, suffering in silence.

"They didn't cry," Mr Yamaguchi said later. "I saw no tears at all. Their hair was burned, and they were completely naked. Everywhere there were burned people, some of them dead, some of them on the verge of death. None of them spoke. None of them had the strength to say a word. I didn't hear human speech, or shouts, just the sound of the city in flames".

As they struggled across the city he and his companions saw bloated corpses floating in the city's rivers, bodies 'bobbing in the water like blocks of wood', and at one point the three men had to wade across a river, parting a floating carpet of corpses to do so.

They spent a sleepless night in an air raid shelter – Japanese civilians had grown used to conventional bombing – and the following morning set out to find out if the railway station was operating.

Again the journey was to bring them all nightmares. 'There were some things I couldn't look at' Mr Iwanaga remembered years later 'internal organs hanging out, the tongue or the eyes hanging loose'.

"We saw a mother with a baby on her back" he went on. 'She looked as if she had lost her mind. The child on her back was dead and I don't know if she even realised. If you have a normal set of nerves it's very difficult to look at something like that'.

Even when they found a train home the terror did not end. At the station Mr Sato managed to lose contact with his two companions, and found himself sitting in a packed railway carriage opposite a shocked young man grasping a pathetic, foul smelling cloth bundle.

'I asked him what it was' Mr Sato recalled years later, 'and he said, "I married a month ago, but my wife died yesterday. I want to take her home to her parents"'. The young man lifted the cloth on his knees to reveal an upturned helmet containing the severed head of his wife.

In spite of all this, and clearly traumatised, all three men reached Nagasaki safely. But while his two companions made their way home,

49

Mr Yamaguchi went straight to the hospital to have his burns treated – while he was there the doctors also found that his left ear drum had been all but destroyed.

What he did not know, and neither did his two companions, was that the nightmare was about to repeat itself.

The ever loyal engineer duly reported back for duty at his factory on the morning of Thursday August 9.

'I was covered in bandages,' he recalled years later. "People could only see my eyes, lips and nose. Until I opened my mouth, my own mother didn't recognise me, but I reported to the director who had sent me to Hiroshima".

'Well, the director was angry. He said: "A single bomb can't destroy a whole city! You've obviously been badly injured, and I think you've gone a little mad". At that moment, outside the window, I saw another flash and the whole office, everything in it, was blown over'.

'The director was shouting "Help me! Help me!" But I realised at once what had happened, it was the same thing as in Hiroshima. But I was so angry with the director that I climbed out of the window and got away because I had to help myself'.

A second American B-29 bomber known as 'Bockscar', had dropped a 25 kiloton plutonium bomb nicknamed 'Fat Man' above the northern part of Nagasaki at 11.02 am. It had exploded 469 metres above the city, and once again Mr Yamaguchi had been barely two miles from the explosion's epicentre.

Of all the hibakusha, he was closest to the centre of both the blasts.

Mr Sato was in another, more distant, part of the shipyard that morning. 'People were asking me what happened in Hiroshima, because they'd heard rumours' he remembered many years later. 'I was just explaining when I saw the flash of light. Instinctively I knew what was happening, so I jumped into the water'. He trod water for an hour. Doing so saved his life. He escaped without a scratch.

Mr Iwanaga, meanwhile, was on a suburban train and although the glass in the windows blew out, he too wasn't hurt.

The same could not be said for Mr Yamaguchi. Although he had only suffered cuts and bruises as a result of the second bomb, the blast had blown off his bandages, leaving his burns exposed to the air.

Undeterred, he managed to get home to his family – but the hospital that had treated him just hours before had been destroyed.

Together with his wife and son, he took refuge in the shelter behind his damaged house, semi-conscious, shaking with a high fever, and afraid that he was about to die. All around him, in the words of the city's Mayor 'not even the sound of insects could be heard'.

'I must have stayed there for a week' Mr Yamaguchi said later. 'I didn't know if it was night or day. Then one day, it was the 15th August, I realised that people around me were crying'. They were listening to the broadcast by 'Emperor Hirohito that announced Japan's surrender'.

'I had no feeling about it' he concluded. 'I was neither sorry nor glad'.

The terrible wounds he suffered on those August mornings six decades ago meant that Mr Yamaguchi – like so many of the estimated 260,000 survivors of the bombs – was to remain in agony for years, in his case until 1961.

'Until I was about 12, he was wrapped in bandages for his skin wounds', his 60-year-old daughter Toshiko – who lives with him still – remembered this week.

Her mother was also soaked in what became known as 'Black Rain' – the radioactive rain that fell after both bombings. Mr Yamaguchi is convinced that it poisoned her and their children.

Yet, typically, after finally recovering from the burns and radiation sickness, Mr Yamaguchi quietly returned to work, first for the United States military government, then as a teacher, before finally returning to Mitsubishi Heavy Industries.

Mr Iwanaga meanwhile became a civil servant in the Nagasaki City Office, and Mr Sato joined the local government of the nearby Amakusa island.

But not one of the three men took part in any of the anti-bomb demonstrations that came to preoccupy some of the other men and women who'd come through the unthinkable ordeal of surviving the explosion of an atomic bomb.

'Afterwards he was so fine, we hardly noticed he was a survivor' says Mr Yamagushi's daughter now, even though he privately called the scars on his arms his 'badge of courage'.

Indeed if you ask Mr Yamaguchi today why he thought he was so lucky: 'He just laughs' she says. 'He just doesn't know'.

What he does know, however, is the suffering each and every one of the survivors had to go through.

It was movingly captured in an account of their plight published barely a year after the bombs were dropped by the American writer John Hershey.

'They still wonder why they lived when so many others died' he wrote in The New Yorker magazine. 'Each of them counts many small items of chance or volition—a step taken in time, a decision to go indoors, catching one streetcar instead of the next—that spared them. And now each knows that in the act of survival he lived a dozen lives and saw more death than he ever thought he would see'.

The gentle Mr Yamagushi saw more death than he ever wanted to see – and lived to tell a story that the world would do well to listen to, and never, ever, forget.

This story demonstrates that we cannot really work in some categorical or separate way with individuals, groups or communities as all these concepts and entities are interconnected and are collectively intertwined with global events and situations. The problems, difficulties, hopes and joys of a single person are linked to psychological, social and universal considerations. No one particular perspective of the human condition is ever adequate in terms of totally explaining or completely addressing the issues that arise in or that are brought to us as part of our work. Nothing exists in a vacuum (perhaps that is why nature abhors them) and everything shapes and is shaped by context. Each one of us is more than the sum of our parts and the world is made up not of 'me' but of 'us'.

Hence State or organisational initiatives that in effect treat communities as the source of problems or the font of resources or the means of general 'betterment' make much the same mistake as those who see social conditions as solely the product of individual psychological dispositions.

When I began my career in youth work the vestiges of a dichotomy between my field and that of community work still existed. It was not uncommon to come across community workers who insisted that they 'did not work with kids' as they 'worked with the community'. I never really grasped how young people were not part of the community or even why young people could not be considered a community in themselves. There was, after all, a 'Black community', a 'Gay community' and a 'senior citizen community'. Could it be perhaps because that would have meant that these professionals would then have to work with them? In the end that philosophy had the means of its own demise built into it, just as community education does.

Putting the problem of its many interpretations aside, which from the start undermine its potential for analysis, and suspending the apparently reasonable doubt about the viability of community as a description of anything much more than a social entity, the boundaries of which are marked out via discrimination and even prejudice, positing it as an ideal situ for education is plainly contradictory.

Education might exist in such a context but it would by necessity be of a restricted nature. While the community feels pragmatically suited as a delivery point for instruction, indoctrination and propaganda, education, by its critical and questioning character, would undermine the fabric of community (the above tale of the journey in and out of 'Gypsydom' might illustrate this).

Community is not adequate as a site of education and education is the antithesis of community. The story of Mr Yamagushi alone calls us to question the rivalries and separations seemingly needlessly erected between people. It reminds us that while we are each of us distinctive, the profound elements of our humanity bind us far more than relatively superficial considerations divide us. The radiation from the bombs that seemed to pursue Mr Yamagushi still lingers in the earth's atmosphere; everyday each one of us takes a minute fraction of it into our bodies.

None of us are entirely separate from what the Hegelians of the mid-19th Century called our 'species-being'. This is the possession of consciousness but not just consciousness of self which other social animals also possess. We are conscious of our essential nature. Hence humans are *sui generis* (have a unique characteristic) in their ability to consider their own species. We also have the capacity to make our own nature an object of thought. The contemplative life is distinctly and exclusively human as this transcends a merely animal individuality in thought. For some (the likes of Feuerbach for example) this meant that human individuality was not just about being oneself but also about being with another. In our immediate situation we are with Mr Yamagushi and perhaps now Feuerbach and they are with us.

This feature of human intellect makes the 'community' a far too claustrophobic locale to facilitate extended thought and development of critique. It is limited in what it can offer in terms of finding out who or what we are at any given time, partly because it is located in one particular place. That is why people have traditionally seen moving away from home, attending university in another city or country, travelling or spending time in the armed services as a rich element in their educational development. This is not so much about geographical movement but the means for the changing of perspective – seeing things from literally a different standpoint. It is, perhaps, a vital factor in energising and extending the critical process (and progress) of education.

Education, beyond a very limited interpretation of the same, hemmed in to the community, will either ultimately smash through its cordons or be contorted and eventually stifled by its restrictions.

As a Gypsy, I must travel or else I am no longer a Gypsy. I now travel with the caravans of the mind along the ancient spice road of education and anyone, regardless of their community origins, can come with me. But in order to explore this universe I have left the community. Life is, in the last analysis, a series of leavings. These are part of our beginnings. To quote the aptly named Alan Jay Lerner, 'I've never seen a sight that doesn't look better looking back'.

What is known 'youth culture' is no more than an overarching term used to commoditise the pirated and processed expression of resistant young people. These expressions are in fact forms of rejection of so called 'youth culture' that is produced not by youth but by those who wish to exploit young people... The 'youth market' is a means of selling reprocessed stolen goods. Then those who peddle this reprocessed pap demand that kids desist from 'pirating' that same stuff, the raw material of which was pirated from youth in the first place – Ward Churchill.

BIBLIOGRAPHY

Buber, M. (1947). *Between man and man*. Kegan Paul.

Chamberlain, W. B. (1941). *Heaven wasn't his destination*. George Allen.

Engels, F. (1934). *Ludwig Feuerbach and the outcome of classical German philosophy*. International Publications.

COMMUNITY AND CONTROL

Is it so much a child needs – the right to have space, and time for exploration, so that each can grow at its own rhythm and become part of society in a natural way...to feel what they feel, to have their experiences accepted as valid, and to be responded to in their own context...to live lives that are their own, not someone else's.

Ask our society that sets each creative child on the conveyor belt, and deals it as it moves along a hammer-blow here and a twist there, till it becomes the anonymous mass component that the State needs, and see society's response...see its priorities...only children, and the sheer brilliance of children, can save each one of us from the sickness and the death that we choose to call living.

–Leila Berg – *Looking at Kids* (p. 144) Penguin 1972

Why is 'community' promoted? What interests are served by the ambition to educate in the community? How does youth work practice in the community relate to wider social considerations and policy agendas? Looking at the work and legacy of Franz Fanon alongside social analysis of contemporary situations, this chapter will explore and critique the conventions of the nature of current theory that claim to explain and justify community education.

The reasoning for, and aims of, education in a community setting is seen by commentators interested in promoting informal community education as a profession beneficial to those on the receiving end of this practice. Simplistically, it is seen to be 'good' because it is 'good'. However, the methods and rationale behind the State supply of informal community education are much more complex than this. Incidentally, it is the State that sanctions and resources informal community education. Even if the voluntary agencies like the Church host the work, funding streams can invariably be traced back to governmental/commercial sources. Some professionals not working in statutory environments might claim not to be sullied by government agenda but they are usually trained on programmes rubber-stamped by State agencies, need to observe national policy or legislation,

B. Belton, Developing Critical Youth Work Theory: Building Professional Judgment in the Community Context, 55–74.
© *2009 Sense Publishers. All rights reserved.*

often receive project funding from various State quangos and/or direct funding from government or local government coffers. Of course, there is no divide between The Church of England and the State in the UK as the monarch is head of both and bishops sit in the highest court in the land – the House of Lords. This, together with tax breaks on property, for example. and the probability that Church of England land would revert to State ownership should disestablishment ever happen, means the Church is as complicit in State activity about as much as any other agency.

A range of social forces is responsible for creating and maintaining the notion of community. To really understand the social role of a community educator, it is necessary to gain some kind of focus on these defining factors. As already argued, just a moment's thought about the nature of community suggests that it is a grouping of people that both holds a group together and keeps others out. To this extent it is a means of discrimination. If we see ourselves developing forms of education that are specific to a given example of this discriminatory entity, the 'Asian community' for example, we might be understood to be promoting a type of apartheid or 'separate development'. This being the case, the promulgation of the notion of community as 'a good thing' does raise suspicions that the concept propagates target areas wherein forms of often covert social control ('education') can be delivered.

John Pilger (1998) gathers together essays on a range of subjects including Burma, Fleet Street, East Timor, Vietnam, the media, and UK politics. Pilger provides his readers with some idea of how British State/government agendas are controlled by big business and the influence of the United States. Ball (1990) demonstrates how education is used to confirm and advance these dominant power structures/elites that seek to control society. This makes sense as education policy. What it is, what it does, and how it is done is dictated, resourced and funded by these concentrations of power.

The material detailed in the bibliography for this chapter develops this notion of social control. If you get a chance to read and/or listen to these writers and thinkers, you might begin to see that informal community education can be understood as having a role within social indoctrination rather than being the 'pure', unsullied form of education that the promoters of informal education seem to insist that it is.

Informal education, its codes of practice, its aims and purposes, is part of the wider, as Foucault might have it, educational control nexus. Community is the site wherein informal education takes place. It is the locale of practice. This work and the training youth workers receive in order to undertake the same is funded directly or indirectly by the State or agencies and institutions that collaborate with the State or even have extensive influence over or within the State. This consideration has a huge impact on what we do in that our activity fits within the wider ambit of control.

Foucault would understand the dichotomy of formal and informal education as irrelevant in terms of the 'global' role and purpose of education. He was not the first or the last person to see how society and the education it funds and resources seeks to create conformity via forms of subtle control.

COLONIALISM AND THE COLONIAL MENTALITY

There are similarities between African experiences of colonisation and life in the local social systems in contemporary British society. As pointed out above, this should not be surprising as the institutions including education that together make up the British State were developed during the time and out of the process of Empire, colonialism and slavery.

The Experience of Informal Education

In terms of the notion of community education, youth work practitioners (even tutors of practitioners) carrying out this function via informal educative strategies do not often seem to be aware of how the confusing collection of activities, aims and policies that are labelled under this 'brand' impact as a whole system within and alongside other national institutional operations such as health, law and so on. However, young people can and do develop a sense of the activity focused on them. Given that the profession reaches only a minority of young people, youth work has relatively little effect on the 'targeted groups'. Perhaps this is a sign that, as a group, young people are aware of what something that practitioners have come to call 'informal community education' is trying to do to them and in response reject/avoid/play along with it. If you put yourself in their shoes this would be understandable.

A person approaches you in the street (a detached worker, for example) letting you know in one way or another that they are there to 'help'/ 'support'/'educate' you. They have presumably come to you with the assumption that you are relatively helpless/unsupported/ignorant. They go on to attempt to 'build a relationship' with and/or 'befriend' you. It might be suggested or made clear that this 'befriending' does not mean that they are actually your 'friend' and it will certainly not extend to invitations to their home, attendance at their birthday parties or weddings, although they might send you a birthday card and not turn down an invitation to your wedding (as this will invade your 'personal space' and not theirs and show their superiors and colleagues how 'close' they are to their clients). It will also be made known, openly or circuitously, that the 'relationship' is to be 'used' to meet organisational/professional/policy ends. This person might say that they want to be 'committed to you' in some way although this commitment will not extend beyond times and days that this person names. They go on to openly ask you to trust them and sometimes refer to their 'unconditional regard or respect' for you. However, because of their patronising attitude and behaviour you doubt this. To you this language sounds a bit like 'grooming' but you give this person the benefit of the doubt as they seem grateful that you are talking to them.

What is going on between you and this paid person will be recorded along with this person's impression of you, your friends and family. This might include the most intimate details and that which you were told was 'confidential'. It is unlikely that you will ever see what is written about you but you, perhaps supported by these recordings, will be discussed with other people usually without your knowledge or permission. Although your name might be changed – Jill to Julie, Mohammad to Imran, your age, gender, school/work and assumptions about your general social, family, class, neighbourhood, sexual background may be shared with others. Words will be used in association with you such as 'care', 'welfare', 'protection' and sometimes even 'love'.

Although you are only seen by this professional for at most a couple of hours a week over perhaps a few months, you will have lay psychological diagnoses made about you despite the fact that those involved may not be qualified, well read or experienced in this field. Most commonly you might be seen to 'lack self-esteem' or 'be attention seeking' although the person making these prognoses actually sought your attention in the first place. Other notions such as 'paranoia' and 'neurosis' might be thrown in for good measure and speculation might go on about you being 'dyslexic' or suffering from 'Attention deficit hyperactivity disorder' (ADHD). You may subsequently be 'treated' according to these relatively poorly informed assumptions while what is being done to you will be called 'skill', 'practice' and even 'art'.

In other places, when you are not present, you will be named as a 'client', 'learner' or 'customer'. In earshot you will be called by your first name or that which those closest to you know you by. Now, is that something you (as a young person) would want to be involved in? Might you rebel against it or feel that these people, who seem to regard you as psychologically or socially 'lacking' and as 'pitiful' while saying they 'respect' you unreservedly, are worthy of your insults?

Fanon and Colonialism

The colonial situation places one group in the role of the oppressed and another group in a dominating position taken by the oppressors. This 'colonial culture' has deep influence on the lives of those bound to it. The relationship between the professional and the 'client group' might be understood to echo some of the characteristics of the colonial situation. On one side are those with all of the formal influence and authority – the adult professional and on the other is the 'client' – often a young person with relatively little formal influence or authority. However, as is the case of the oppressed in the colonial situation, they may have a deal of latent or potential informal influence and authority.

In looking at the colonial system in Africa, the seminal Martinique-born psychiatrist, philosopher, author and revolutionary Frantz Fanon (1925-1961) argues that the colonised are labelled by, and dependent on, the definition of the coloniser. He discusses the way in which a group of people become 'defined' by another (an outsider group) to the extent that their whole 'self' and understanding of their humanity is dependent on that definition. The professional, operating in the community, is constantly involved in defining people or validating categories bestowed on, for example, 'target groups'; the 'excluded', those 'at risk', Not in Employment, Education or Training (NEET) or with 'special needs'. Having been conscripted to a category, individuals and groups access approved social resources and are referred to and treated according to their assigned label.

Fanon points out that once people become dependent on this definition that is made by others (the outsider), generally without their knowing input. The defined (colonised) person begins to live in order to fulfil that definition. They become as the oppressor would have them become:

Man is only human to the extent to which he tries to impose his existence on another man in order to be recognised by him. As long as he has not been effectively recognised by the other, that other will remain the theme of his actions. It is on that other being, on recognition by that other being, that his own human worth and reality depend. It is that other being in whom the meaning of his life is condensed. (Fanon 1952, p. 217)

This process is energized by the fact that most of the resources for life are mediated by the oppressing group. This is powerful motivation for the colonized to accept their given definition – any resources that are provided are made via that definition. This process should be familiar to the professional working in the community wherein the client ('native') can access resources by way of their acceptance of the professional's definition of them (as funding target).

Fanon outlines what might be thought of as the 'colonial mentality', through an analysis of the 'colonial neurosis' (Fanon 1952, p. 83-108). For Fanon:

> *The central idea is that the confrontation of 'civilised' and 'primitive' men creates a special situation – the colonial situation – and brings about the emergence of a mass of illusions and misunderstandings that only a psychological analysis can place and define.* (Fanon 1952, p. 65)

According to Fanon, colonialism establishes a relationship between oppressor and oppressed that is founded on an assumption of the inferiority of the oppressed group and superiority of those who make up the oppressing elite (Jinadu 1986, p. 28-30). He argues that this relationship becomes part of the mentality of the oppressed to the extent that they are only able to perceive themselves as they are portrayed or understood to be by the oppressing group. It can be seen to be the case that this analysis is applicable to the relationship between professionals and their 'client groups' within the community. The professional goes into a community seeking to 'educate' or 'inform', to 'better', 'enable', 'empower' and so on which are essentially actions based on 'deficit models'. They are founded on a supposed lack and are invariably applied via 'intervention' without anyone in the 'target community' requesting such an incursion.

For Fanon, the oppressed become trapped by these definitions of their selves. At the same time the oppressors become convinced of their role and consequently habituate it. Fanon argues that this is a dehumanising process. The oppressed are not regarded as fully human by themselves or the oppressor. They define themselves and are defined as 'the other' ('the client'?). Only the oppressor is wholly human.

This is the fundamental problem with calling someone an 'adolescent' or part of a 'nuisance group'. Their identity as a human then takes on a secondary status as one is firstly a type (e.g. NEET) with traits that differentiate and alienate the individual from the whole i.e. the rest of the 'community'. They might have an Anti-social Behaviour Order (ASBO) for example. The only way out of this for the individual is to attempt to move back into the mainstream through forms of social compliance and conformity to particular norms. Fanon argues that the mechanisms of adaptation and imitation within the colonial relationship are often very subtle. Certain norms are established and imposed to which the oppressed group are then required to conform. For Fanon these mechanisms are, in the main, covert but they can also be overt and deliberately instituted with sanctions stipulated by the oppressing group.

The professional in the community is employed and deployed to validate and extend socially accepted forms of behaviour. Being employed by the State or its agencies, professional activity is about extending the influence of those that sponsor, fund or pay professional groups and not subjective notions of 'the good' or for the 'benefit' of individuals or specific groups. This is what brings professional interaction close to the relationships fostered in the colonial situation (see also Illich 1983).

Adaptation to the colonial situation by imitation, being achieved by covert (informal?) means, feels like spontaneous activity as it takes place within the confines of everyday life. The overt forms of adaptation are openly induced so that in terms of work with young people, the Connexions Service might be thought of as a relatively overt means of achieving adaptation relative to informal education. For Fanon:

> *The arrival of the white man in Madagascar shattered not only its horizons but its psychological mechanisms... an island like Madagascar invaded overnight by 'pioneers of civilisation,' even if those pioneers conducted themselves as well as they knew how, suffered the loss of its basic structure... the landing of the white man on Madagascar inflicted injury without measure. The consequences of the interruption of Europeans onto Madagascar were not psychological alone, since, every authority has observed, there are inner relationships between consciousness and the social context.*
> (Fanon 1952, p. 97)

This process is not too far from the relationship between professional 'client groups' and the State. The 'invasion' of the community, by a whole range of professional forces of the State, the police, 'educators', medical workers and so on, is undertaken in order to oblige/encourage/persuade those in the community whose behaviour is deemed in some way 'anti-social' to comply with social norms as defined by the media and the State. Unless these individuals and groups conform, they will remain confined within characterisations such as 'at risk', 'the excluded' and so on and suffer the consequences. Fanon states:

> *I begin to suffer from not being a white man to the degree that the white man imposes discrimination on me, makes me a colonised native, robs me of all worth, all individuality tells me that I am a parasite on the world, and that I must bring myself as quickly as possible into step with the white world.* (Fanon, 1952, p. 98)

According to Fanon the 'urge' to become like the white 'cultured' oppressor leads the 'acculturated' colonial subject to despise those 'less fortunate' in his society. This might be understood as being similar to the negative feelings that the adult world seems to have towards young people or youth culture. Thus we – us and those we work with and among – can be understood to be bound up in a colonial situation that can only be compounded by the constant development and validation of problem or deficit categories. The concept of the 'client' as the 'other' needs to be challenged by an analysis that can demonstrate that such groups arise out of the social and economic fabric of the State. They are invented and energized for the purposes of ruling elites and do not have an independent existence outside of this. As far as young people and other 'client groups' are concerned, this amounts to a discourse of decolonisation.

HACKNEY INSIGHT

The following was written by Nicholas Estephane, an experienced youth worker practicing in East London. As a *youth of yesterday* he sees himself as entering the field of youth work to *pass on knowledge to the youth of today*, who may, like himself *once, have been unaware of the greater forces or the 'matrix' in which we all live*. Nicholas devotes his practice to the *hope that we can all work through it with success!* It is arresting to see how his experience not only echoes Fanon's position but elaborates on the same. His narrative discussion that follows, looking at the meaning and purpose of informal education delivered in the wrapping of community education, suggests that the ethos of colonisation, far from disappearing with the demise of Empire, exists like scar in the body of our experience, wherein there is a restless tension between stated purpose and the seemingly unpreventable function of the social form. I am grateful to Nicholas for his consent to use his work that animates theory via a practice perspective.

Trevor Phillips (the Chair of the Equality and Human Rights Commission) has declared that, *We live in a society where black maleness is in some ways the definition of failure* and it does seem that media coverage together with attitudes that have been prevalent in education for decades, has left many with the impression that there is at least a lack of expectation with regard to the performance of young black men within the British educational system.

The young men I have worked with over the last few years have, overwhelmingly, had negative opinions about, and responses to, their own communities and wider society. Their expectations about the influence and reaction of social networks outside friendship and family groups are correspondingly low. I have also found that the communities these young people live and go to school in have low expectations of them, while most young people feel that there is more conflict than cohesion within their communities. They understand the educational system to be more or less, informally or formally, organised to set them up to fail.

As a community worker this situation has caused me to ask more and more 'what is the real motive behind community education?' Is it really a means to bring people together or does it rather create divisions between people? Does a community need professional advocates or educators to come in and 'teach' it about itself, to learn about their own community? I do not follow a syllabus therefore what do I teach the people I come into contact with? Am I proposing that I can teach them about themselves, their culture, their identity or their values?

Can education of itself boost confidence and self-esteem? Do we need education? Perhaps education just might be the route of all evil? It has certainly been my experience that many school teachers have low expectations of young black men, seeing this group as almost necessarily bound to lead a life of crime and dysfunction. This, together with the negative stereotyping this can help give rise to, seems to place young black men at a disadvantage before they can really get a grasp on what is going on.

Perhaps it is the role of the community educator to challenge all these issues by 'teaching' young people that they hold the key to their own success in life? This sort of function might be understood as a text book example of community education or empowerment. Community empowerment is said to be about people and government working together to make life better, 'skilling-up' more people to be able to influence decisions about their communities, encouraging individuals and groups to take responsibility for tackling local problems, rather than expecting others to do this for them.

The contention behind all this is that government cannot solve everything by itself, nor can the community. According to government rhetoric things can be made 'better' only when 'we' work together.

The three key factors to community empowerment are:
- Active citizens – people with the motivation, skills and confidence to speak up for their communities and say what improvements are needed.
- Strengthened communities – community groups with the capability and resources to bring people together to work out shared solutions
- Partnership – bringing public bodies together, working as 'partners' with local people.

This vision for 'empowering communities' was originally set out by the then Home Secretary, David Blunkett MP, in a key speech in 2003. What we need to bear in mind here is that Mr Blunkett had, and has, no real idea of what goes on within so-called 'dysfunctional' communities such as those I work in. In fairness, Mr Blunkett himself is from a so called 'underprivileged' background. However, the misfortune of Mr Blunkett's early years in industrial Sheffield is certainly not the same as a young black male in the inner city 'murder zone' of Hackney. Moreover, despite all Mr Blunkett's early deprivations, he became successful. The young black men I work with suffer similar or worse misfortune, but few of them go on to write autobiographies about their life as cabinet ministers. Why is that?

Why is there so much emphasis on community education and empowerment in areas such as Hackney? When one compares the City of Sheffield to the Borough of Hackney in terms of negative press over the years, Hackney is in the 'Bad News Premiership' compared to the Steel City. Perhaps the large amount of scrutiny Hackney comes under might be due to the fact that the position of ethnic minorities in Hackney attracts more interest than the blue collar issues of Sheffield?

Looking at the tactics of community education, which are said to be put in place so people and government can work together to make life 'better', it feels necessary to point out that these strategies appear to arise out of the assumption that life is so bad for those living within these communities that interventions need to take place in order to 'educate' and make life 'better'. It is intriguing that no real gap exists between the identification of the problem and the response. Indeed they might be thought of as the same thing!

This feels like 'colonial' intervention. Historically, European colonisers went into Africa with the intention to 'educate' people on the basis of an assumption that these people had a need for 'civilisation', 'education' and 'government'. They were understood and portrayed as having nothing of this sort of their own and indeed they were seen not even to have a culture. The colonisers were fired by the assumption that the ancient civilisations of Africa needed a 'better' life. The action and the reaction went hand in hand, just as it seems to in Hackney today.

The era of colonialism is comparatively recent history and its echoes and legacy persist in the life of institutions that were informed by and confirmed the nature of Empire.

Of course, just as colonised regions were overall worse off after colonisation, communities treated in much the same way in the present era often appear to be detrimentally effected following professional 'interventions'. These frequently bring with them increased surveillance, the promotion of a negative focus in order to justify the expenditure incurred by professional incursions and a subsequent rise in insecurity among older residents and young people.

The agenda of modern day policy, having quite a few similarities to colonial policy, does cause one to question the purpose and nature of informal community education. While the government believes that it alone cannot achieve the ambitions of community empowerment or community education, that same government has the means to impose the rule of law and take away rights. This hardly makes sense. Perhaps the real reason that the government can't achieve its ambitions for communities without conscripting communities themselves to their cause is that the communities it targets have not asked for any intervention. Just as no African invited the colonisers to Africa and Africans had to be recruited to the cause of the colonisers in order that the colonisation could take place.

Why is it that communities are seen as unable to 'better' their own situation? Perhaps the government uses the 'working together' tactic as a covert means of keeping certain communities at a particular level. If government have worked 'tirelessly' with communities such as those in Hackney to 'better' their current situation, why does the situation seem to go from bad to worse or remain completely stagnant? Why do the majority of young people within these communities feel that they are effectively negatively targeted? Why do young people within the community feel as though they are segregated as opposed to being integrated with other groups within the community?

The government claims it is working towards community cohesion, declaring that cohesion must happen in all communities to enable different groups of people to get on well together. A key contributor to community cohesion is 'integration' which is seen as something that must happen to enable new residents and existing residents to adjust to one another. This ambition is built on the premise that people from different backgrounds have similar life opportunities and equal knowledge of and access to their rights and responsibilities. It assumes that people trust one another and have faith that local institutions will act fairly. The rhetoric of community cohesion has it that for people to live together effectively they should,
– have a shared future vision and sense of belonging
– have a focus on what communities have in common
– recognise the value of diversity, and
– a strong and positive relationship between people from different backgrounds should exist.
All this is far from happening. In fact, the situation seems to be the complete opposite.

If the government works with communities in order to address issues that affect them, why do people feel segregated? Perhaps these plans work to prevent communities coming together. While policy focus looks to cultural, racial and ethnic cohesion and integration, is society in reality divided along the lines of social class and status? We are indeed a multicultural society, but to what extent?

In a 2005 speech Trevor Phillips spoke of his concerns that Britain was 'sleepwalking its way into segregation' in his speech he said:

Some areas are becoming fully fledged ghettoes. These are black holes into which no one goes without fear and trepidation and from which no one ever escapes undamaged.

Take Leicester for instance. Many people there live in what social scientists call ghettoes, two thirds of people here are from a single ethnic group. Some parts of the country could become fully fledged ghettoes like those in the United States.

Phillips also claimed that integration was unnatural and had to be imposed on people from above:

Integration is a learned competence like maths or driving a car, it is not instinctive… If we all lived separately but knew, liked and mixed with people of different races and backgrounds, we might regard that as a tolerable compromise. But we know that human nature is not like that.

At the time these comments caused something of an uproar, particularly from those living within communities in Leicester. It was thought that Phillips was aiming his comments at Muslim communities. But if we look at what Phillips said with an 'open mind' one might ask if perhaps individuals living within these so-called 'urban ghettos' are there as a result of systems and agendas of other forces. Those who live within the urban ghetto may well indeed want to better their position but are caught up in the workings of policy systems or procedures. It feels too easy to blame human behaviour for a community failing or refusing to integrate.

The young people I work with often have extremely high aspirations. Their main cause for concern is the education system and how they feel it fails them. If the government works towards the 'betterment of the community' as they suggest, why is it that schools in the so-called 'urban ghettos' go from bad to worse or close down completely? Why is it that schools in Chelsea and Westminster have a higher success rate than Haringey or Hackney? Why is it that there are comparatively few 'social housing' estates within London Boroughs such as Chelsea? Is it because all those from the Muslim and Black community have a passionate dislike for Chelsea? The football team perhaps, but if people within the 'urban ghettos' had the opportunity to 'progress' might they emancipate themselves from their current social position and rub shoulders with the 'Premier League' of Chelsea?

At the time of writing, unemployment among those aged 16-24 has hit a fifteen percent high. Statistics show that the rate among 16 and 17 year old school leavers could be as high as twenty eight percent. At the same time as university fees are set to rise. We are therefore looking at a generation of young people growing up facing a future of mounting debt and unemployment!

Most young people now have no option but to work and study full-time, which naturally causes stress. This in turn has an impact on their education but they cannot give up their job as they need to survive. There are some young people who would like to go to university but are apprehensive about having no means to pay university fees. The consequence is that they incur thousands of pounds of debt with the possibility of no job at the end of their studies.

For young people to make a future for themselves they should not be put under this stress but assisted to focus on their studies. I certainly felt obliged at the age of 16 to stop going to college and seek employment as I struggled to get by financially. But if 'community betterment' is a genuine aim should we all, no matter what our social standing, be given the opportunity to a decent and equal education?

Why is there so much negative press around young people and education within the 'urban ghetto'? Who made the assumption that they do not want a school, college or university education? Have we considered the fact that they may indeed want such opportunities? Moreover if the government 'work tirelessly' in the cause of education, why are young people only funded to degree level? Do young people not aspire to study any further? What about funding for a Masters and PhD? Are these available for the 'Premier League' only?

The field of educational theory seems to converge on the conclusion that all human beings should be entitled to an education and benefit from the passing on of knowledge, in order to fulfil their life potential and exceed their limits and expectations. (John Dewey (1938), W.E.B. Du Bois (1973), Barack Obama (2004), Malcolm X (1965 and 1992) and Booker T Washington (1903) are relevant here).

Booker T Washington summed up the 'true spirit' of community education in an address he made with regard to race relations and equality. He wanted to bring the 'Black' and 'White' races together, in order to encourage the cultivation of 'friendly relations' between them. Washington's theory was that the Negro should consider the interests of the community in which s/he lived, rather than seek alone to please or serve the interests of someone who lived a thousand miles away from him/her:

> *In this address I said that the whole future of the Negro rested largely upon the question as to whether or not he should make himself, through his skill, intelligence, and character, of such undeniable value to the community in which he lived that the community could not dispense with his presence. I said that any individual who learned to do something better than anybody else, learned to do a common thing in an uncommon manner, had solved his problem, regardless of the colour of his skin, and that in proportion as the Negro learned to produce what other people wanted and must have, in the same proportion would he be respected'.* (Washington, 1901: 98)

Washington speaks here of an instance where one of his graduates had produced two hundred and sixty-six bushels of sweet potatoes from an acre of ground where the average production was only forty-nine bushels to the acre. Today's issues have become more complex than this but in terms of community education and 'community spirit' in keeping with this notion, it describes the backbone of community education or perhaps what it could be. To start from 'within' and work our 'way out'. Isn't this the 'true spirit' of community education? To build up what you have, work with it, make it stronger, prepare it, 'come together' in order to create a 'solid foundation' that will be strong enough to hold any amount of intensity. Washington went on to say:

> *These white farmers honoured and respected him because he, by his skill and knowledge, had added something to the wealth and the comfort of the community in which he lived. I explained that my theory of education for the Negro would not confine him for all time to farm life, to the production of the best and the most sweet potatoes, but that if he succeeded in this line of industry, he could lay the foundations upon which his children and grandchildren could grow to higher and more important things in life.* (ibid.)

The true notion of community education is to build up what you have, use your resources however small, start from somewhere!

Marcus Garvey speaks of education as being the experience and knowledge that is gained through everyday life. Garvey was a strong believer in people 'knowing themselves' in order to be fully effective within their community and society. Garvey's theory of education also suggested that the Negro race should 'emancipate' themselves from 'mental slavery' and look not to 'western teaching' but look to the 'East' and Eastern civilisation as they would find more purpose and meaning there. A strong and influential leader, Garvey believed people should know themselves as they hold the key to their own success:

To be learned in all that is worth while knowing. Not to be crammed with the subject matter of the book or the philosophy of the class room, but to store away in your head such facts as you need for the daily application of life, so that you may the better in all things understand your fellowmen, and interpret your relationship to your Creator. You can be educated in soul, vision and feeling, as well as in mind. To see your enemy and know him is a part of the complete education of man; to spiritually regulate one's self is another form of the higher education that fits man for a nobler place in life, and still, to approach your brother by the feeling of your own humanity, is an education that softens the ills of the world and makes us kind indeed. Many a man was educated outside the school room. It is something you let out, not completely take in. You are part of it, for it is natural; it is dormant simply because you will not develop it, but God creates every man with it knowingly or unknowingly to him who possesses it, that's the difference. Develop yours and you become as great and full of knowledge as the other fellow without even entering the class room. (Garvey, 1986: 9)

For the most part, such ideas are unjustly, perhaps outrageously, ignored in youth and community work training. Aspects of Washington and Garvey are more than appropriate and relevant while having the content to take thinking on. Perhaps that tells its own story! They help to expose a deeply colonial ethos in the trajectory of community education. Poor standards of schooling causes education to fail young people while social conditions created by consistent State offensives are then made the target of so-called ameliorations that in fact both confirm and further enhance individual, group and community stagnation and alienation. The ghettos created undermine the gradual social and genetic 'blending' and are then assaulted by 'integration mercenaries', professional social mechanics who are given the impossible job of harassing, pushing and herding the now defensive and alienated mono-ethnic populations of these enclaves into a monstrous homogeneity that can only ever exist as the figment of a deranged bourgeois nightmare.

For all this, community education may have as its operational focus a school or community centre or it may have no specific location but be an activity of a village or neighbourhood. It may be primarily concerned with learning or with community development or community action. Inevitably and properly, its form derives from the social, cultural and historical context within which it is being practiced and from the needs of the people involved. I believe that the root of the solutions to a community's problem is contained within that community. Therefore, when the likes of a professional community educator or ' skilled facilitator' intervenes in order to find out what the needs of that community are, it becomes a little more complex.

We need to be sensitive in the way in which we approach communities. I say this as I believe failure to approach in a thoughtful and considerate manner may cause upset and hostility from those within the community. How do I know how it really feels to walk in the 'tight shoes' of those within that community when my own shoes fit perfectly? Even if I use my 'skill' of 'dialogue' as an 'informal community educator' to 'draw out' what the community needs, it does not necessarily make me part of that community. This is the point where it becomes complicated in that the line between education and colonisation becomes thin. We risk at least patronising people. How does Gordon Brown know what it feels like to be a 16 year old Black boy living in Hackney in a two bedroom flat with his 'single mum' and two little sisters. That boy might one day hope to go to University but his mum works only two days a week.

What we should be talking about is how we reach an integrated society, one in which people are equal under the law, where there are common values of democracy rather than violence, the common currency of the English language, honouring the culture of these islands, like Shakespeare and Dickens – Trevor Phillips

SAVING GRACE

Youth work (as opposed to informal or community education) can be a fairly straightforward process although necessarily one carried out with sensitivity and thoughtfulness. It is also a practice that can be undertaken without seeing people in deficit.

Grace was a youth worker in the 1950s. Her dad, a Jamaican soldier who served in the First World War, had come to East London in the early 1920s and married her mother, 'a mouthy Silver Town girl like me' as Grace described her, who worked in a local pickle factory and 'on the side' sang and played the banjo in local pubs.

When I first started working with a group of kids, they, as is natural, would each, or sometimes as a pair, go in different directions. I didn't tell them what to do unless something was dangerous. I understood that I was not their teacher. Never wanted to be. But I seem to have

had the knack of going with them so that we, eventually more or less together, went in a particular direction, to what I think most of them seem to have found...a better place.

Youth work I don't think is about being an educator or a leader. It is a job where you make room for leaders to emerge and for leadership to be shared...it is a kind of socialism...youth work, at its best, well I think, is political. Although you might never mention politics, people, if you can let them, 'make action' and 'take action' and they become aware of their own influence and authority. Isn't that more than education? Isn't that something close to the tools of liberation? Ha ha...

I don't think I ever consciously tried to 'educate' anyone; except myself – would be pompous to say I did wouldn't it? Education probably happened between me and the kids I worked with but to 'try' and educate someone is probably self defeating anyway isn't it? I mean, if people want education it tends to be cooperative don't it? One person asks for education and the other person gives it if they've got it. But the person educating gets educated from the people they are educating...ha ha ha. Otherwise it aint education...it's just instruction or training! Like you train a dog. Do people 'educate' dogs?

Two way thing is education. But I wasn't in education, although it may have been a 'side-effect' – I have though seen hundreds of kids, in one way or another, liberate themselves (sometimes a lot, sometimes a little) by working together. We also had a lot of fun. Being and working with other people is what fun is mostly isn't it? It is also what politics is; not me looking after everyone, but everyone looking after each other, making decisions about themselves and between themselves.

I don't know what power is, but in people, unity is strength. Why? Because in that unity there is influence; collective influence is authority and having authority means that you can take control of your life and your environment. Without authority, what have you got? Only what someone who has authority is prepared to give you. And that won't be their authority ha ha! If you want authority mate, you gotta make it and take it! I think, I hope, that's what came out of the youth work I did for the kids I worked with.

Denise Rayner is currently an Area Youth Service Manager working in Bedfordshire. It is remarkable how much she agrees with the above although there are clear differences in approach and perspective. Commenting on Grace's position Denise told me,

I think we are still social educators, we do make room for potential leaders to emerge, but I feel we make room and open up opportunities for all who engage with us to realise their potential (dependent on how self limiting they wish it to be!). We can help with the self limitations through challenging them with new experiences and increasing their confidence but we need to realise this is also dependent on other 'influential' factors they may have in their lives.

Absolutely, education can and should be co-education. We are co-educators; we learn from each other. There should be no hierarchy in learning. Freire makes reference to that in 'Pedagogy of the Oppressed'.

Yes, being and working with other people can be fun (and hopefully mostly is) however that is not always the case. Idealistically, politics could be 'everyone looking after each other, making decisions about themselves and between themselves', however, in reality, it does not appear to be that way. Capitalism is embedded deep in the fabric of our society and it has grown deeper through 'globalisation' of national economies. Personally I see politics (whether you are Blue or Red) as being 'controlling'; 'a means to an end', 'profit and greed being considered far more important than humanity'! Very sad but true.

Unity is indeed strength and within unity there is influence and collective influence is authority; and having authority can mean taking control of your life and the environment around you (to an extent) but again I think we need to be realistic and manage expectations when working with young people. Yes, we can 'liberate' them and ensure they have control over their lives and their environment but we need to also inform them of the way the world around them works, both in terms of societal pressures and controls, politically and how to work around the policies, and laws to ensure they gain 'true' authority.

I totally agree with the last point: 'Without authority, what have you got? Only what someone who has authority is prepared to give you'. If you are not aware of the 'law' and legislation, how can you enable and empower young people to fight for their rights and advocate on behalf of them?

As youth workers I see a major contributory factor to our success with young people, not just around the relationship building, but also how we engage with them to encourage and stimulate their motivation to connect with whatever activity the work is focusing on. Offering different and challenging activities helps to tease them out of their 'comfort zones' and realise, although the challenge may be hard, what an amazing feeling it is to achieve and take part. It isn't about winning, it's the taking part and giving it your best that counts. The belief another person has in you to achieve – I feel that truly helps to motivate the young person and therefore assists in questioning the mindset of the other influences in their lives

While Grace looks back on her career in youth work with a sense of buccaneering optimism, informed mostly it seems by a sense of enthusiasm and belief, perhaps enlivened with a measure of faith in the possibilities of political consciousness, Denise demonstrates a more cautious outlook, tempered by an informed realism and an apparent (understandable) loss of enchantment with the political process. But she probably has more definite ambitions for the young people she works with relative to Grace. Grace seemingly felt able to work relatively unselfconsciously although she has a considered philosophical standpoint that remains feisty, fresh and confident. Denise has an intelligent understanding of her role which she seems to use to work 'between the cracks', diligently developing a means to work with compromise for what she sees as the benefit of her clients.

These two perspectives, both from experienced, committed and able practitioners, as comparatives say much more about the changing nature of the field than perhaps anything else. They reveal a path from where we have come from to where we are. But let's not be easy prey to nostalgia. Over the generations not much has changed in terms of the function of the State, but what might be called the 'professional cultural memory' has informed us. We have, maybe, become more aware of the nature of things. This, along with the increased surveillance of conduct and the discouragement of risk taking with young people has caused a more circumspect approach. Perhaps also the increased emphasis on the covert nature of informal education (we work to an agenda not always shared with our clients) has caused youth workers to extend surreptitious responses to management, adjusting our 'scripts of practice' in the face of intrusive direction and the undermining of professional judgement.

The building of 'safe environments' has now become a prime duty of youth workers although to many teenagers, 'safe' seems to equate to 'boring'. One can't help but wonder what the emphasis on providing safe 'shelters' presupposes about young people. 'Safe' of course is another word for 'secure' which itself is a word used in the penitentry realm. Perhaps if a group can be convinced that they are victims they are more likely to opt for 'guarded' premises, preferring their behaviour to be obseved and recorded than face what professionals subtly, perhaops mostly unconsciously, imply is the threatened ostracism beyond the 'safe' boundry defined and patrolled by the professional. In an environment so haunted by the shadow of the young person as gudgeon, an unhappy sufferer from their own age category, which possibly allows for a simplistic role identification for the 'professional as protector', it is maybe an optimist who might determine to understand youth agencies more as havens for which people celebrating their youth might spring from rather than fearfully huddle in.

...believe half of what you see
... and none of what you hear
Marvin Gaye – 'Heard it Through the Grapevine'

BIBLIOGRAPHY

Ball, S. J. (1990). *Foucault and education*. Taylor and Francis.
Belton, B. (2007). *Black routes*. Hansib Publications.
Caute, D. (1970). *Fanon*. London: Fontana Press Ltd.
Chomsky, N. (2000). *Chomsky on Miseducation*. Rowman & Littlefield Publishers.
Cleaver, E. (1971). *Soul on ice*. Panther.
Dewey, J. (1938). *Experience and education*. Touchstone.
Du Bois, W. E. B. (1973). *The education of black people: Ten critiques, 1906–1960*. The University of Massachusetts Press.
Fanon, F. (1952). *The wretched of the earth*. Harmondsworth: Macgibbon and Kee/Penguin Books Ltd.
Fanon, F. (1961). *Black skins, white masks*. Pluto Press.
Garvey, A. J. (1986). *The philosophy and opinions of Marcus Garvey, or Africa for the Africans*. Majority Press.
Illich, I. (1983). *Deschooling society*. Harpercollins.
Illich, I. (2000). *The disabling professions*. Marion Boyars.
Jinadu, A. L. (1986). *Fanon: In search of the African revolution*. London: KPI Limited.
Kruger, A. (1990). *Community education in the western world*. Routledge.
Martin, T. (1983). *Marcus Garvey, Hero*. The Majority Press.
Mills, C. W. (1959). *The sociological imagination*. Oxford University Press.
Obama, B. (2004). *Dreams from my father*. Random House.
Orwell, G. (2004). *Nineteen eighty-four*. Penguin Classics; New Ed.
Pilger, J. (1998). *Hidden agendas*. Vintage.
Washington, B. T. (1901). *Up from slavery*. Cosimo, Inc.
X, M. (1965). *The autobiography of Malcolm X*. Penguin.
X, M., et al. (1992). *Malcolm X speaks*. Andrews Mcmeel.

WEB SITES

www.guardian.co.uk/society/archive/journals
Darcus Howe (race relations)
Trevor Phillips (equality and race relations), (education)
The Prison Industrial Complex (Audio CD, AK Press – 2000)) featuring the voice and ideas of Angela Davis
Propaganda and Control of the Public Mind (Audio CD, Alternative Tentacle - 1998) a recording of the Harvard Trade Union Program by Noam Chomsky
Manufacturing Consent: Noam Chomsky and the Media (2009) - Bfi DVD

COLLECTIVENESS AND CONNECTIVENESS

Uncertainty and expectation are the joys of life. Security is an insipid thing

–William Cowper

We have considered the logic of 'colonising' the feeling of community for the purposes of social control. This 'hijacking' of sentiment is understandable as it makes sense for the State or power elite to undermine the potential of any form of solidarity that might be used to subvert or resist its aims. One way to undermine potentially dissident elements is to absorb them into the whole. This has happened to the trade union movement in Japan and the United States. What was once a threat to the dominant elite in those countries is now part of the same. For all this, what we might understand as 'solidarity' or expressions of social accord seems always to be in a state of renewal (it keeps on happening). This coming together of people with like interests or feelings of commonality appears to be part of what might be thought of as our 'social being'. How this happens is not adequately expressed in the theories relating to community. Academic explanations cannot quite capture how we tend to 'coagulate' into human (and humane) coalescence but we can express something of this experience.

What follows is a narrative relating to the nature and character of 'community' and how it manifests in biography. As such it questions theoretical/academic models to adequately help us understand the 'relatedness' of community.

I used to go to reserve games at West Ham's Upton Park ground. They don't do that anymore, the pitch is saved, in the main, for first team games. I started going when I was about five or six. My four or five mates and I would play for the Hammers against Spurs, Arsenal or, for some reason I can't recall, Santos in the FA Cup final in Castle Street, waiting for gates to the North Bank to be opened at half-time allowing us to 'flood' into the near-deserted edifice. The North Bank stood where the Centenary Stand now overlooks the Irons' sacred turf and from its forsaken, yawning entrails, we'd watch snatches of the

B. Belton, *Developing Critical Youth Work Theory: Building Professional Judgment in the Community Context*, 75–86.

game between mimicking match days, crushing up together behind a single barrier, shouting warnings like, 'stop bumming me' and loudly questioning, 'who's pissed in my pocket?' while imploring the claret and blue second string to, 'Coom-yon-uuu-Iiiiionnnnzzz'.

Other distractions from viewing West Ham's twilight regiment of future and past being pulverised (memory's a bitch) included games of 'he' and standing directly in front of lone pensioners. We would look at them in counterfeit shock as they pelted us with a comfortably predictable deluge of verbal filth. We would also mime 'crowd riots' (a challenge for such a small group with a collective age of 35) or line-up one behind the other and 'do pushers', sending us, a little ball of humanity, tumbling down the concrete hill that was the terraces of our North Bank home.

Another favourite pastime was congering up and down the near uninhabited hardness, chanting, to the tune of the Seven Dwarves classic, 'Hi-Ho!'; Mile End, Mile End, Mile End, Mile End, Mile End.... (such performances could go on for a near twenty minutes and occasionally more than an hour). This was the mantra of the 'Mile End Mob', a collection of youth gangs that would meet at Mile End underground station to become West Ham's travelling buccaneer army of the 1960s. These young weekday rivals from Stepney, Canning Town, Whitechapel, Dagenham, Hornchurch and all the 'villages' north of the River, east of the Tower, an area still then pock-marked with the ravages of the blitz and continuing poverty, would, come the next first-team game, crush together onto the North Bank to renew their collective allegiance to the mighty Hammers. One day we would join their ranks and carouse around the urban wastelands of England celebrating being 'we'.

But on a winter's evening, as the floodlights of the Boleyn Ground broke through the icy mist that shrouded London's docklands, maybe 500 dawns into the 'swinging' decade of the last century, we were far too young to be part of those pilgrimages. Our ambitions were set on becoming 'Snipers', the under-13 (more or less) cadet corps of the 'Mile End'. It was just after singing and swaying to the Sniper hymn, Snniiiipuzzz, Snniiiipuzzz that I got knocked unconscious.

In time with our homage, our choir pointed towards what was then the enclosure where visiting supporters would be directed, the despised South Bank (that would eventually metamorphose into the Bobby Moore Stand). The future would transform the South Bank into the 'home end', in a rather lame effort to break the cult of the 'Mile End' and control match day trouble. The tactic was to mark the end of the MEM, but it gave rise to its more vicious, malicious successor, The Intercity Firm, for whom violence was an end in itself; sadistic sickness replaced aggressive solidarity as the hard boys moved on and hit-and-run yob culture ruled; a sad and abstracted individuated rabble spurned out of, and reflecting the Thatcherite sect-of-the-self.

Our 'Sniperian' sonnet had been going some moments when the ball was murdered by the chest of West Ham's Johnny Byrne. The stained sphere fell, seemingly as slow as a leaf, to receive a mighty belt from the Byrne right boot. The shot screamed towards the goal, but with the lightest kiss atop the away side's bar, the oscillating orb cannoned on...straight towards...me!

*I don't know how, when or why I decided that I wound head the ball back at Byrne, but spreading both arms wide, I pushed my compatriots aside and flung myself towards the on-coming missile. I saw it spinning in the air, turning like some mad banshee, it screamed its coming and I knew I would make contact; I would meet this challenge and connect with **MY** team. I would be totally Hammered!*

The last thing I remember before leather met cranium was marvelling that so much turn could be applied at such great force. Then the lights went out, at least in my diminutive nut anyway. In the expanse of my childish unconscious, I had a little dream wherein Percy Dalton (the peanut man) was arguing with the West Ham manager Ron Greenwood about the state of the buses. Ron was calling in Yogi Bear to arbitrate, him being smarter than the average bear, when illumination was restored. I awoke looking into the face of Johnny 'Budgie' Byrne. Like, England international, most expensive footballer ever, Johnny fucking Byrne! 'You okay, Sonny?' he asked looking concerned.

My modest firm were standing round in awe, little Colin Jones, the amazing two foot Trinidadian, smallest giant in the East End, was mutely holding out a crumpled piece of paper and a blue betting office pencil. Byrne had jumped out of the fantasy realm of the pitch into the stark reality of the North Bank; he had crossed the divide of dreams and run up the terraces to where I lay. 'Yeah' I said, trying to pretend that my flight down twenty feet of terraced inflexibility had been deliberate. I was planning on saying something like, 'I do that all the time, John', when he remarked, 'Good header' and gave a little chuckle as he helped me to my feet. 'Thanks' I replied with all the nonchalance I could muster.

Budgie signed Tony's scrap of putrid papyrus and trotted back down to where the other players were, quite rightly, looking up at him from the other side of reality. That autograph would be with Colin forty years on. He carried it into eternity in the top pocket of the suit he wore as he was cremated in a little Catholic chapel in New York after a long battle with an evil illness.

My first conversation with Johnny Byrne would not be the last, but our next chat would be separated by the tumult of my teenage years and John's combustive reign in world football. But we never really parted. As I followed him and his West Ham, we were all Hammers. Incited by Bobby Moore, our coming was felt like the distant thunder of Zulu army jogging, inextricably, across the veldt. At the best of times, just when the opposition thought it had heard the last of the Irons, the portentous presence of Moore would coagulate in the middle of the park and the buzz of swiftness around the ball would start, eliding out space and enveloping it, Byrne, Hurst, Boyce, Sissons, Brabrook would dazzle, dizzy and confuse to weave the Hammers back into contention. Sophisticated in assault out of defence, passing along the ground with intoxicating accuracy, rarely did the ball take flight; darting runs carried it to rock the enemy like lightening bolts from the claret and blue. A collusion of deft passing and on-the-ball skill was their only authority.

That West Ham side had the ability to generate an idyll of football. Never had so much soccer anticipation been stirred to be so thoroughly sated. Those were the days of 'we' when 'us' was all there was that mattered.

WEBS OF SIGNIFICATION

This narrative captures something of what it is to be part of a greater whole – an identity and/or a collective connected through a spirit of solidarity. Herein there is a well of empathy, support, nostalgia, help, challenge, fun, excitement, refuge, escape, sympathy, joy, sorrow and hope. It is the epic of our socio-emotional lives set in experience, animated by our desires, drives, urges, fantasies and wishes. It is the interpersonal flux that makes life worth living. This collective connectedness is close to the notion of Geertz's 'webs of signification' (Geertz 1973, p. 30) and I am going to align this with ideas about a cultural 'worldview'. Worldview, for Braid, informs personal 'perceptions, actions, ideas, and interpretations and therefore influences the dynamics of interaction in the world' (Braid 1997, p. 39). It is fundamental in the generation of perceptions of identity and difference. For him,

A person who approaches or interprets his or her world in a similar way is perceived to have a similar identity. Someone who behaves and interprets the world differently is perceived to have a different identity. (ibid.).

This description is of something more than community but probably most people reading this will be able to relate to it. From this standpoint, I am going to look at the influence and importance of the appreciation of 'webs of signification' in the local social setting as well as our potential part in them as professionals with an ambition to educate.

BUILDING WEBS

What I am going to refer to might be thought of as a rather unusual model of community mapping that is primarily, in practice, concerned with the non-duplication of services or what might be thought of as a type of resource management. To an extent, community mapping is a technique or method that, it is said, can be applied in a generic way i.e. it is supposed to be relevant in all locations and at all times. However, I will introduce a perspective that is a bit more organic than this harnessing of something that is inherent to our function as human beings.

As we have seen looking at Habermas (above) communication is central to human functioning. Verbal communication is made up of a number of forms. As an informal educator, you may see yourself 'engaging in dialogue' – a kind of artificial conversation in which the 'educator' has approached another person or other people with what is often a covert agenda – ideas and aims not necessarily shared with the person(s) who the ideas are about or the aims are for. Informal education is premised on the practitioner having objectives that the 'target group' do not necessarily know about. The person or people are turned into 'clients', although the words 'you are my client' are hardly ever uttered. As such what is called 'dialogue' is more, as a 'professional tool', a clandestine interview or interrogation than an everyday conversation, although once more, this is unlikely to made clear to targeted individuals or groups.

For the most part, our ordinary, reflexive verbal communications are not commandeered or colonised by professionals and **used** by them to meet organisational outcomes or State ends. In the main talking develops between people in the process of chatting, discoursing, arguing, rowing, gossiping, yapping, chattering, debating, discussing and sometimes through dialectic. All of these forms of verbal communication are used by us as individuals to receive and give, share information. This information could refer to ourselves and/or others, be about what we do or the nature of the world also a means of expressing ideas. However, perhaps the very height of human interaction is dialectic – the energetic, passionate exchange, development and transformation of ideas – a kind of critical response to experience. This process might be understood as the means by which we construct our 'worldview'; the way we generate and build on our identity and our place in and the meaning of our existence.

In short, we are what we are through our interactions with others. We grow through and by our interactions. As such, it follows that we shrink or limit our growth while we minimise our interaction with others. This stands the test of experience. When individuals, groups and communities become isolated, they tend to become self-destructive both biologically and psychologically.

Most of us, in youth and community work, using informal educational techniques, despite our boasts about being the experts in terms of communication and dialogue, work in relative isolation. We might talk to other workers in our own or related fields, maybe social workers and teachers, sometimes people involved in criminal justice and police, but few of us would be able to chart a web of such interactions. By this I mean we might talk to a police officer one day and a teacher next week but it is rare that we chat to a police officer and a teacher about the same thing and even rarer at the same time. Here I am not talking about 'patch meetings' or case conferences. These are essentially business meetings between welfare/education providers. They are a bit like the dialogue that some informal educators see themselves as indulging in, what Braid calls 'superorganic' and therefore not essentially about generating 'emergent personal constructs'.

To know an area, we need to know not just what is going on in that vicinity in order to supply things that are not already there. We need to know what people do, how and why they do it, and to allow them to know similar information about us. For example, a local vicar wanted to attract young people to her church, very basically to save their souls. However, these young people were not all that interested in redemption or 'the good news'. So she opened a coffee bar in the crypt, found a pool table and a TV and started a club. As such didn't say much about saving souls, but emphasised the relative 'safety' of the facility and the 'fun' that could be had there, lots of young people turned up. Down the road there was a café where many of the young people had previously hung out. It too had a pool table and a TV but the owner didn't have the same set of aims as the vicar although his aims were a bit more 'open'. No one thought he was opening his premises just because he wanted people to 'have fun' or 'be safe'; primarily the owner wanted to make money and that was understood.

Here, superficially, we can see services being replicated, but is this the case? If we go back to Braid you might see that there is something quite different going on. It is not 'what' we are doing that matters but the interactions that are going on. It is 'how' we do things that makes a difference. How we do things facilitates (or hampers) the building of our 'webs of signification'. You might see a hint of this in the material that opened this chapter.

This does not mean, however, that I can just sit with what I'm doing and say it is different to anything else and therefore justifiable. What the vicar did had an impact on the café owner and they are now in competition. If the café owner is a good capitalist, he will look to counter the vicar's USP (unique selling point) but he can't undercut her sweet prices. The vicar sells close to cost price and allows the young people to play pool for free. All the café owner can do is offer more resources, so he buys a smart new pool table, a bigger TV, and installs video games. Competition nearly always involves a resource or service war.

We are, I suggest, constantly involved in this type of competition. At the moment it is most noticeable in funding. Funding tends to be about who is best in making the case and filling in the forms rather than getting resources to those most in need. The 'superorganic' takes precedence over the nurturing of 'emergent personal constructs', ideas developing out of personal experience, feelings and perspectives. But why was it that the vicar and the café owner did not speak to one another about what they both wanted to do? What might have stopped them from cooperating?

The following recollections might give you an idea of what the emergent personal constructs are and have been for Jenny who some years ago shared her wartime memories with me.

JENNY'S WAR

Dad went to war after Dunkirk. We had stood by the riverbank at Woolwich and watched as, for the first time ever, the ferry turned fully downstream to lead a Thames Armada to France. Tough little tugs were followed by sedate steamers, brine-stained traders and a flotilla of Thames Barges; the great plethora of colour of their sails made an imprint on my mind. The River Police ushered along pleasure boats that had tottered down from Richmond and Kew and a whole phalanx of little yachts and ancient fishing boats that once were part of the great Barking fishing fleet. The biggest surprise of all came last. Not to be left out, the massive Thames Docks Dredger, 'The King Arthur', a great creaking steel edifice, slowly brought up the rear. Our road of water, our river, was a tributary of hope that day and dad had to follow too.

I was very little but Mum used to take me down to the hop fields and I would do what I could but mostly played with the other kids. It was a hot day. I remember Mum laughing with the other women, all talking about their husbands, one of whom was my dad, who were away at the War. Mum smiled and sang, 'Charlie is my darling' and all the other women joined in as they pulled at the vines. I tried to join in, 'la-de-da-ing' where I didn't know the words.

I remember it began to get dark, just before we heard a faint 'brumming' sound. It was like a sort of regular turning of an engine with a slight pause between, 'brumm, brumm'. As it got louder everyone was looking up at the sky. I remember like a big black cloud moving over the sky. I thought it was thunder but this was the first big raid on London. My home.

I knew it was the Germans when my mum scooped me up and ran with everyone else to the trenches dug around the hop gardens. As we jumped into the ditches it was almost dark. I clung to Mum but recall being more fascinated than frightened. Everyone's eyes were fixed on the great cloud as it began to cover the sun. In the fading light we saw two small, slim silhouettes rising up into the air – one in the west, the other in the east. I knew they were planes – 'ours'. The little crowd of women in the trench were quiet, watching the little fighters, expressionless, silently stunned by the sight as they arched up into the foreboding cloud.

But they seemed to hang in between heaven and earth for a moment, seemingly pausing. At that moment there was a roar that seemed to break just over our heads and a plane with RAF markings zoomed no more than a few feet above us. I heard one of the old women whisper loudly, with awe-like passion, 'Spitfire'.

We watched the plane fly just above the hop poles and turn at tremendous speed back towards us. As he began to gain height, heading to join his siblings that were still waiting for him, the little terrier of an aircraft threw a victory roll over the hop gardens and in one elegant movement, the three tiny angels flew up in unison, disappearing into the blackness that now covered the sun.

When we got home we went down to our street to find a great pile of rubble where our house had been. I remember rummaging with

Mum through the rubble looking for anything we might salvage but everything seemed shattered. I found a record, remarkably unscathed, that I kept for years afterwards: Pee Wee Hunt's 'Twelfth Street Rag' and Mum found a picture of Dad in his uniform. That was it. All we had in the world. I was about to cry but Mum seemed fine. 'Let's go and see Aunt Mary,' she said, 'we'll have a nice cup of tea,' and off we marched. Up Prince Regents Lane towards Plaistow, where Aunt Mary lived. I loved to go round Mary's. Uncle Bob, like dad, was away at the War but her kids were great fun for me to be with. Dolly is about my age but Jim and Emma are a bit older. Anyway, we were near to Mary's when the air raid warning went.

Mum decided that we would continue make for Mary's and share her shelter. We were about fifty yards from our destination when a German fighter seemed to appear out of nowhere, flying straight down Prince Regents Lane. It seemed to be coming for me and Mum! It was like a great black bat, flame came from both its wings and bullets were bouncing up shards of road all around us. Mum pushed me to the ground and leapt on top of me but I saw the face of the pilot who was firing at us through a gap between her and the pavement. I saw his goggles and his grimacing mouth. Why was he shooting at us?

The next thing I remember was sitting in Mary's shelter with Mum and Mary's kids. Mum was shaking violently but not crying and was holding a big mug of tea. Mary was frantic, standing up and sitting down, saying, 'Fucking bastards, fucking evil bastards!'

We went back to Kent for a few days with Mary and her kids. There was little work to do but there was some clearing up. We stayed in a little cottage, much more luxurious than the usual huts. Our farmer was always nice and I think he was helping us out, given what had happened. We'd been there a while when we saw more bombers heading for London. We had watched a German plane come down a few miles away and everyone in the fields cheered as it plummeted to the earth somewhere beyond Goudhurst. As I followed the smoke churning up into the sky, I saw a parachute floating down in a diagonal towards where we were staying.

Mum and Mary worked quite late that day. The hop gardens were now clear and the poles flat. It was a bit like the day after the Christmas decorations come down. The fields were grey and naked. They looked vulnerable and sad. I remembered when we had come down at the start of the season. The gardens had been heavy and green, all jolly

83

and waiting for us. The smell of the ripe hops had been overpowering and they were full of great dragonflies that every now and then zipped passed us like little roaming rainbows.

As we walked back to our cottage we sang. We were all singing 'Ten Green Bottles' when we saw the German airman hanging from a telegraph pole. His parachute had caught the top of the pole and he was hanging from it. He had three pitchforks pinning him to the pole, one through his neck, one in his chest and another in his stomach, but his face looked very peaceful. He had short dark hair. Looking back, I guess he was very young, maybe no more than early 20s. Mum pulled my face into her as we passed. I heard Mary say 'serves the fucker right'.

We came back to London and just walked into an empty place in Sampson Street, Plaistow and we saw out the Blitz and the War there. We spent many nights in the Anderson shelter at the bottom of the yard and, over the War years, Mum must have made and drunk an ocean of tea.

I never thought the Germans were evil. The one who had fire on mum and me had just looked scared. Once, many years after the way, while on holiday in Rome, I saw a painting of St Sebastian. He was tied to a tree, his body filled with arrows. It is a terribly sad picture. Sebastian looks so helpless. Ever since it reminded me of that young German hanging on the telegraph pole at the end of that wartime Summer in Kent. At the same time, often, when I hear the word 'Spitfire', I cry.

The best times were when Dad came home. He would often bring home food 'negotiated from the cook-house' as he used to say. This was taking quite a chance as he would have been severely punished if found out. Once he brought home a whole conger eel, wrapped around his waist under his army greatcoat. There must have been quite a few suspicious exchanges of eye contact in the train carriage he came back to London in.

Of course, the greatest time of all was when my dad came home for good. It was a week or so after V.E. Day. We spent the first few days as a threesome, and then I went down to Southend for the day with Aunt Mary and Uncle Bob and their kids (Bob had got back a few weeks prior to the first victory celebrations). I asked why Mum and Dad weren't coming with us and Mary told me that they had to 'rebuild their memories' that day. I didn't understand at the time but when we got back to Sampson Street and knocked on our door, Mum answered it in her dressing gown and no slippers! I had never seen my mum, not even during the blitz, go anywhere without shoes or slippers on.

Having looked at Jenny's situation it might be informative to ask yourself what role, if any, a professional informal educator might have in relation to the situations the speaker found herself in. How would the professional 'map' this situation? How might this compare to Jenny's 'maps' built partly out of her experiences? Was she 'being educated'? Or was what happened to her more related to considerations like awareness, insight, understanding, revelation and epiphany? Can all these levels of human comprehension be subsumed under the single heading of 'education'? If so, why would we have so many labels for the same experience?

What Jenny was doing was letting us into her worldview and telling us something of how it was made, arising, as it did, out of her webs of signification. Something the vicar and the café owner above did not do.

On a mass scale, Hitler's National Socialist State exemplified something of the same conflict relationship that existed between the vicar and the café owner. It undermined the production of modern art and instead promoted classical or traditional art as the apex of aesthetics. It literally outlawed jazz. War was promoted as the most powerful means of national and social development.

We may, as youth and community workers, be well placed to attend to the development of worldviews, to influence the building of webs of signification perhaps through our encounters with and part in the emergence of personal constructs. As you might have understood from Jenny's situation, this is something much more complex perhaps than the mere project to educate.

If you look closely at your work and the overall picture of the professional practice of youth work in relation to community education, can it be said that we are in fact just educators? Yes, we might use what passes for the 'skills' of informal education but in practice does the trajectory of our interactions with those we work have a much wider brief?

As the two narratives included in this chapter demonstrate, our lives are played through a whole range of activities and emotions. Perhaps education is just one aspect of our life, one that many are unsuited for or do not want to any large extent. What seems more certain is that most of us look for and seek to experience fidelity, solidarity, friendship as well as the giving and taking of care to develop our webs of signification. This search may involve education but these uniquely humane faculties are also the seedbed of a much wider field of human interaction. As our ability to think, develop, store and manipulate knowledge might affect and be affected by our illusions, dreams, imaginings, hopes, fears, desires and lusts so education is but one channel for our deeper intellectual capacities; the abstract products of mind. 'We are such things as dreams are made of...'

Conflict is the gadfly of thought. It stirs us to observation and memory. It instigates to invention. It shocks us out of sheep like passivity, and sets us at noting and contriving – John Dewy

BIBLIOGRAPHY

Anderson, N. (1961). Diverse perspectives of community. *International Review of Community Development*.

Braid, D. (1997). The construction of identity through narrative: Folklore and the travelling people of Scotland. In T. Acton & G. Mundy (Eds.), *Romani culture and gypsy identity*. Hertfordshire University Press.

Geertz, C. (1973). *The interpretation of cultures*. Basic Books.

Kasler, D. (1988). *Max Weber*. Polity Press.

Parkin, F. (1979). *Marxism and class theory*. Tavistock.

Schmalenbach, H. (1977). *Communion – a sociological category*. In G. Luschen & G. Stone (Eds.), *Herman Schmalenbach: On society and experience*. Chicago University Press.

Weber, M. (1978). *Economy and society* (Vol. i). University of California Press.

CHAPTER 6

RACE AND ETHNICITY

Great ideas often receive violent opposition from mediocre minds
                                                    –Albert Einstein

This chapter will explore the concepts of race, ethnicity and culture, while questioning the relevance of these forms of categorisation and ask why and how they are sustained and used. According to Sollors (1989),

> *Ethnic groups are typically imagined as if they were natural, real, eternal, stable, and static units. They seem to be always already in existence. As subject of study, each group yields an essential continuum of certain myths and traits, or of human capital. The focus is on the group's preservation and survival, which appear threatened. Conflicts generally seem to emerge from the world outside of the particular ethnic group investigated.* (ibid., pxiii-xiv)

I will examine ethnicity as a form of identity, and ask you, as you read the following, to ask how and why it affects, shapes, and defines the direction of youth work practice.

WHAT IS ETHNICITY?

Notions of 'blood', hereditary, race and theories of 'origin' or lineage are central within the discourse surrounding identity. However, Stuart Hall, who has made a massive contribution to the discussion of ethnicity, has warned,

> *Since cultural diversity is, increasingly, the fate of the modern world, and ethnic absolutism a regressive feature of late-modernity, the greatest danger now arises from forms of national or cultural identity – new or old – that attempt to secure their identity by adopting closed versions of culture or community, and by the refusal to engage with the difficult problems that arise from trying to live with difference.* (Hall 1992, p. 8)

B. Belton, Developing Critical Youth Work Theory: Building Professional Judgment in the Community Context, 87–99.

This echoes Hall's earlier contention that,

>*...the boundaries of difference are continually repositioned in relation to different reference points.* (Hall 1990, p. 227)

However, identity is couched in aspects of life-style and 'self-ascription'. Identity or ethnicity can thus, it seems, be 'culturally' adopted. The resulting confusion within the collective analysis of identity is compounded by the lack of consideration of the role of economic, social, inter-group and interpersonal factors within the development of the ethnic paradigm of identity.

The following looks at the notion of ethnicity and identity but it will also seek to understand, in the context of the contemporary social and economic environment, what the label of ethnicity explains about individuals, groups and society. I will argue that ethnic categories are socially constructed, adopted and ascribed and seek to examine the social purpose, maintenance and relevance of ethnic categories in contemporary society. As Stuart Hall has commented,

>*...one has to remember that the issue of race provides one of the most important ways of understanding how this society actually works and how it has arrived where it is.* (Hall 1981a, p. 19)

This will be undertaken by suggesting, from a Weberian perspective, that social action contributes to the process of ethnic categorisation. The confusion surrounding ethnicity, identity and the reductionist position that portrays groups of people arising out of a 'blood nexus' – that describes identity via a discourse relating to hereditary and diasporic factors – obviates the importance of an examination of the social, economic, inter-group, and interpersonal factors impacting on the development of identity and ethnicity. There is a need to understand what this categorisation means for those categorised and society in general.

The theme throughout echoes Stuart Hall's hagiography for 'cultural studies' which emphasises fractures rather than continuity.

>*In serious, critical intellectual work, there are no 'absolute beginnings' and few unbroken continuities... what we find, instead, is an untidy but characteristic unevenness of development. What is important are the significant breaks – where old lines of thought are disrupted, older constellations displaced, and elements, old and new, are regrouped around a different set of premises and themes...* (Hall 1981b, p. 69)

FROM RACE TO ETHNICITY

According to Hannaford (1996) the concept of race is

...of extremely recent origin...it wasn't until the French and American Revolutions and social upheavals that followed that the idea of race was fully conceptualised... (p. 4-5)

Banton (2000, p. 51-63) argues that the idea of race has moved from a pre 18th century interpretation of an expression of descent to a 19th century concept, based in an erroneous scientific movement, relating to human types (see also Stepan 1982). This construct was to be discredited in the 20th century confining the language of race to fringe political activity. In everyday discourse the seemingly less biologically determinist notion of ethnicity has replaced race as the defining category of human taxonomy (Lieberman, L., Littlefield, A. and Reynolds, L. T. 1975, p. 49-50). However, the notions of race and ethnicity have both been deployed as distinct forms of categorisation.

Ideas of race have mostly been used to exclude others from privilege, whereas a shared sense of common ethnic origin has been used as a basis for the creation of an inclusive group (though a group will be the more strongly constructed when it is based on several kinds of social distinctiveness and not on ethnic origin alone).

Ethnic groups are created when a consciousness of shared ethnic origin is the primary basis for the creation of an inclusive group. Racial categories are created when beliefs about biological differences are used to exclude persons from equal relations. (Banton 1987, p. 199)

This emphasises the social nature of ethnic categorisation. There is little that is biologically predetermined. Here ethnicity can be understood as a product of social interaction, although Malik (1996, p. 174) points out that there is no consensus about the meaning of ethnicity. He cites Rex's position that race and ethnicity have no objective reality (1986, p. 175). This is confirmed by Sollors (1989) who maintained that,

Ethnic groups are typically imagined as if they were natural, real, eternal, stable, and static units. They seem to be always already in existence. As subjects of study, each group yields an essential continuum of certain myths and traits, or of human capital. The focus is on the group's preservation and survival, which appear threatened. Conflicts generally seem to emerge from the world outside of the particular ethnic group investigated. (ibid., p. xiii-xiv)

This appears to hold true in relation to a number of groups who are portrayed in the literature as essentially a consistent 'natural, real, eternal, stable and static' phenomenon, that are victims of 'host' communities beyond themselves. It is hard to understand why the general debate relating to ethnicity should be so moribund, but as Sollors states,

> *Assimilation is the foe of ethnicity; hence there are numerous polemics against the blandness of melting pot, mainstream, and majority culture (even though these polemics themselves surely must have cultural dominance at this moment in history). The studies that result from such premises typically lead to an isolationist, group-by-group approach that emphasizes "authenticity" and cultural heritage within the individual, somewhat idealized group – at the expense of more widely shared historical conditions and cultural features, of dynamic interaction and syncretism.* (ibid., p. xiv)

I intend to look at the theoretical causation of ethnic theory but for the moment I will begin to examine the nature of ethnic categorisation.

WHY ETHNICITY?

The requirement for forms of separateness and authenticity runs through the literature relating to ethnicity. However, Sollors questions this 'taken for granted' attitude in relation to the ethnic label.

> *Are not ethnic groups part of the historical process, tied to the history of modern nationalism? Though they may pretend to be eternal and essential, are they not of rather recent origin and eminently pliable and unstable? Is not modernism an important source of ethnicity? Do not new ethnic groups continually emerge? Even where they exist over long time spans, do not ethnic groups constantly change and redefine themselves?* (Sollors 1989, p. xiv)

The instability of ethnicity is inextricably linked to social conditions that given groups and individuals find themselves in. Contemporary situations give rise to ethnic formulations that compliment and are necessary to these situations. Sollors suggests that the literature betrays a certain ancestry.

> *What is the active contribution literature makes, as a productive force, to the emergence and maintenance of communities by reverberation and ethnic distinctions? Are not the formulas of 'originality' and 'authenticity' in ethnic discourse a palpable legacy of European romanticism? How is the illusion of ethnic 'authenticity' stylistically created in a text? Despite all the diatribes, is not the opposition*

between 'pluralism' and 'assimilation' a false one? Does not any 'ethnic' system rely on an opposition to something, 'non-ethnic', and is not this very antithesis more important than the interchangeable content (of flags, anthems, and the applicable vernacular)? (ibid.)

Such questions mark out the peculiar, abstract nature of ethnic categorisation. In a sense more is attached to the notion than might be guessed through a straightforward sociological dictionary definition. It was not until 1953 (according to the Oxford English Dictionary) that it really came into general usage. Malik (1996, p. 174) argues that, 'ethnicity' is a "fairly post-war word". He cites Huxley and Haddon as being the first to suggest that the concept of 'race' should be replaced by the notion of 'ethnic group'. For Huxley and Haddon, this allowed for the study of social difference without the political connotations evoked by ideas relating to 'race'. These are further elaborated by McLoughlin (1994, p. 80).

Malik (1996, p. 174) argues that ethnicity, like race, "is a term that is used in a fairly promiscuous way", but little agreement exists as to the meaning of the word. Although he makes the case that, in the main, race refers to, "differences created by imputed biological distinctions" while "ethnicity refers to differences with regard to cultural distinctions" (ibid.), he sees the definition of ethnicity as tautological, in that an ethnic group is that which is defined as an ethnic group. However, it is this that allows humanity to be segmented into distinct categories without suffering the accusation of racism.

The term 'ethnicity' avoids objective, biological categories, but does so by introducing subjective distinctions. Malik argues that in usage, the concept of ethnicity cannot be discerned from that of race (ibid., p. 176). He refers to Chapman (1993, p. 21) who sees 'ethnicity' being 'race' with the biology expunged. Malik argues in favour of this proposition suggesting that ethnicity includes the biological ideas of race as a factor in identity. For him, ethnicity "bridges the gap between racial and cultural definitions of social difference." (Malik 1996, p. 176). Ethnic differences in British society are expressed via values and behaviour (cultural norms) so instead of going from the starting point of racial differentiation to the cultural differences 'inherent' to that race, the analysis moves from cultural differ-entiation to the racial end point. The sum of both processes is the same – racial differentiation and ethnic groups retaining a range of essentialist, homogenous identities. This gives credence to the idea of multiculturalism which overestimates the autonomy and homogeneity of particular ethnic groupings while underestimating the amount of interdependence of cultural forms.

Culture, for Malik, has taken on the role of race being something that one is regarded to have been born into. Consequently, a cultural history includes the power of biology. Culture represents an exclusivity set in a common past that includes some and excludes others. The past is made teleological and determinist. It has power over the 'now' through notions of 'roots' and tradition (ibid., p. 186). Malik cites the work of Scruton (1990, p. 187) to further his position.

> It (culture) denotes a continuity across generations, based in kinship and intermarriage, but supported by a consciousness of common descent. This common descent creates the obligation of inheritance: we must receive from our forefathers that which we also pass to our children. Only the idea that inheritance is entirely **biological** rather than cultural renders the concept suspect to those of open mind.

For Malik, the stripping away of biology from the concept of race, seeing through the focus of cultural inheritance has created a new discourse of race amenable to the post-Nazi period. Cultural debate has reincarnated the assumptions of racial thought but in a guise that can accommodate the cultural exclusivists and help them to deny their racism.

The above analysis argues that the notions of culture, ethnicity and race are interchangeable as analytical notions. However, for the purposes of analysis, I will explore the notion of ethnicity, because in contemporary social discourse it seems to be the most prevalent of the terms used to categorise and separate human beings into discrete 'types'.

This opens ethnicity and culture up to the same accusation made against race by Montagu (1997), who asserts it is, "man's most dangerous myth".

Following the combination of Malik's argument and Montagu's analysis it appears that the notions of culture and ethnicity are, like the concept of race, problematical taxonomies. However, the persistence of the social propensity to ethnically, racially and culturally categorise continues. This might be seen to arise out of a drive to cleanse or alternatively to equalise, a desire to 'celebrate' difference or oppress those who are deemed to be 'different'. The moment a distinction is made, it can be used in both positive and negative ways but it is in making difference an aspect of notoriety that starts the ball of categorisation rolling.

ETHNICITY – A SOCIAL CONSTRUCTION

Ethnicity might be best understood as a socially constructed phenomenon. This position is affirmed by the conclusions of many theorists, for example,

Ethnic identity and difference are socially produced in the here and now, not archaeologically salvaged from the disappearing past. Smith (1992, p. 513)

This fits with Gilroy's outlook that sees identity in a constant state of flux, regeneration and reformation.

I am excited, for example by Rakim's repeated suggestion that 'it ain't where you're from, it's where you're at'. It grants a priority to the present, emphasising a view of identity as an ongoing process of self-making at a time when myths of origins are so appealing. (1993, p. 201-2)

And although, as Calhoun puts it,

We know of no people without names, no languages or cultures in which some manner of distinctions between self and other, we and they, are not made ... "

He goes on to support Gilroy and Smith.

...Self-knowledge – always a constriction no matter how much it feels like a discovery – is never altogether separable from claims to be known in specific ways by others. (Calhoun 1994, p. 9-10)

For Calhoun, the complex nature of ethnic identity formation cannot be dealt with through straightforward, reductionist arguments. The problem of ethnic identity is that no single heuristic device is able to explain the whole phenomenon. Overall ethnic and cultural differences can be understood as a function of 'group-ness' appearing as a form of distinction and opposition or discrimination. However, the existence of a group is not necessarily a reflection of cultural difference. The existence of an ethnic group implies ethnic relations and these logically involve two main collective parties – they are not unilateral. Identity is a matter of inputs and outputs.

This goes along with the social constructionist and oppositionist models of ethnicity, that ethnic groups are what people believe or think them to be. Cultural differences mark 'group-ness', they do not cause it or indelibly characterise it. Ethnic identification arises out of and within interaction between groups. This is in line with Coser's position that,

An ethnic group is not one because of the degree of measurable or observable difference from other groups: it is an ethnic group, on the contrary, because the people in it and the people out of it know that it is one; because both the ins and the outs talk, feel, and act as if it were a separate group. This is possible only if there are ways of telling who belongs to the group and who does not, and if a person learns early, deeply, and usually irrevocably to what group he belongs. If it is easy to resign from the group, it is not truly an ethnic group. (Coser 1994, p. 91)

This position is confirmed by Jenkins describing the basic social anthropological model of ethnicity. He makes the point that,

- ethnicity is about cultural differentiation... identity is always a dialectic between similarity and deference;
- ethnicity is centrally concerned with culture – shared meaning – but it is also rooted in, and to a considerable extent the outcome of, social interaction;
- ethnicity is no more fixed or unchanging than the culture of which it is a component or the situations in which it is produced and reproduced;
- ethnicity as a social identity is collective and individual, externalised in social interaction and internalized in personal self-identification.
- (Jenkins 1997, p. 13-14)

On the basis of this Jenkins states:

...neither culture nor ethnicity is 'something' that people 'have', or, indeed, to which they 'belong'. They are, rather, complex repertoires which people experience, use, learn and 'do' in their daily lives, within which they construct an ongoing sense of themselves and an understanding of their fellows. (ibid., p. 14)

Woodward elaborates on this.

I have argued that identities are forged through the marking of difference. This marking of difference takes place both through the symbolic systems of representation, and through forms of social exclusion. Identity, then, is not the opposite of, but depends on, difference. In social relations, these forms of symbolic and social difference are established, at least in part, through the operation of what are called classificatory systems. A classificatory system applies a principle of difference to a population in such a way as to be able to divide them and all their characteristics into at least two, opposing groups – us/them...self/other. (Woodward 1997, p. 29)

It can be seen that this analysis echoes Weber (1922) seeing adoption or implication of a race or ethnicity as a kind of secondary response to other social phenomena.

...race creates a 'group' only when it is subjectively perceived as a common trait: this happens only when a neighbourhood or the mere proximity of racially different persons is the basis of joint (mostly

*political) action, or conversely, when some common experiences of members of the same race are linked to some antagonism against its members of an **obviously** different group.* (Weber 1922, p. 385)

And further,

...ethnic membership does not constitute a group; it only facilitates group formation of any kind, particularly in the political sphere. On the other hand, it is primarily the political community, no matter how artificially organized that inspires the belief in common ethnicity. (ibid., p. 389)

According to Weber, race or ethnicity arise out of a group experiencing, 'some antagonism against its members'. It 'facilitates group formation of any kind, particularly in the political sphere'. Ethnicity seems to be, for those who follow the Weberian/social constructionist analysis (and this includes Barth (1969) and Hughes (1994, p. 91-96).), the product of inter-group agitation or dissatisfaction. This is exemplified in Weber's notion of social closure, which can be seen as an elaboration of oppositionalism.

ETHNICITY AS IDENTITY

Foucault's view of identity formation is consistent with a social construc-tionist view.

The individual is not a pre-given entity which is seized on by the exercise of power. The individual, with his identity and characteristics, is the product of a relation of power exercised over bodies, multiplicities, desires, forces. (Quoted in Gordon 1980, p. 74)

Subjectivity and the body are at the centre of Foucault's thinking and his genealogical method.

A form of history which can account for the constitution of knowledges, discourses, domains of objects etc., without having to make reference to a subject which is either transcendental in relation to the field of events or runs in its empty sameness throughout the course of history. (ibid. p. 117)

This confirms Solomos and Back's position that:

...ideas about race and ethnicity have been constructed and recons-tructed in specific national political environments... this makes it impossible to conceptualise discourses about race and identity as monolithic and unchangeable. (1996, p. 99)

For Foucault, the forms of knowledge unusual to our contemporary way of knowing are restricted by what he called 'conditions of possibility', or 'episteme' from which they arise and which they reproduce. An episteme is the 'total set of relations that unite, at a given period, the discursive practices that produce epistemological figures, sciences and possibly formalised systems' (Foucault 1972, p. 191). From this perspective, the body, and the identity it carries, is a construct emerging out of a particular episteme. As such, it is 'the effect of forces and a problem demanding explanation.' (Butchart 1998, p. 14). Groups we refer to as 'ethnic' are thus specific and complimentary to the episteme. Ethnic identity is not a consistent, practically unchanging, timeless phenomenon.

Wray and Newitz agree with Foucault to the extent that they see identities, in part, arising out of historically specific social systems. For them, as social groups produce physical objects characteristic in terms of their ideas about ritual, ideology, and interaction, they also create idealised notions of identity that appear to fit a specific way of living. They maintain that:

It has often been the task of critics and theorists to "read" such objects and identities as a way of gauging how a particular culture works and why. Recently, cultural critics…have suggested new ways to understand human society in the dialectical relationship between material objects and idealized concepts: that is, they each offer a way to use Marx's early formulation of base and superstructure as a means to interpret cultural change as it is occurring. (Wray and Newitz 1997, p. 6-7)

Wray and Newitz consider the 'white trash' identity to be what Sherry Turkle (1995) called a 'test-object', (quoted by Wray and Newitz 1997, p. 7) something that can be utilised to consider the nature of identity in contemporary society. Ethnicity might be thought of in a similar way. The creation and maintenance of ethnic identity can tell us something about the society within which that identity is propagated. Ethnic identity can be understood as arising out of, 'the dialectical relationship between material objects and idealized concepts' offering 'a means to interpret cultural change as it is occurring'. (ibid., p. 6-7)

RACE, COMMUNITY AND MYTH

Giving credence to the race is putting faith in what from the above can be seen to be an illusion, a mere invention but it is not just that. Racial boundaries have a pedigree in the attempt to rationalize slavery; the enslaved could be enslaved because firstly racial categories were devised and out of that a hierarchy of race established. So racial divisions have their genesis not only in inherently flawed theory but in the most appalling and disgraceful era in human history; the notion was generated out of a scramble to justify a barbarism. To knowingly abet this is to align with a pernicious lie. At the same time championing its progeny, ethnic and cultural categorisation is no more than an attempt to camouflage the function and meaning of race with dysphemisms.

As such the effort to build and 'foster' communities around ideas of 'culture', 'race' of 'ethnicity' could at best be interpreted as veiling a defective construct with a myth. It seems a great deal of our time as professionals is, quite rightly, spent 'promoting diversity' and 'celebrating difference', but what of our commonality? It seems there is much more that unites us than divides humanity. Today the naming of difference is 'celebrated' but as history is witness, tomorrow this naming can become the means of condemnation, oppression and persecution. Categorisation all too readily invites the creation of supposed hierarchies. One can't help but wonder if racial, ethnic and cultural categorisations (that were perpetrated at least as much by the eugenicist justifiers of slavery and the racists of the past and present as the 'celebrants of difference' in the contemporary period) are in fact 'Man's Most Dangerous Myth' and as such provide community educators with a challenging task.

Study without reflection is a waste of time; reflection without study is dangerous — Confucius

BIBLIOGRAPHY

Appiah, K. A. (1996). *Color conscious*. Princetown University Press.

Banton, M. (1987). *Racial theories*. Cambridge University Press.

Banton, M. (2000). The idiom of race. In S. Back & J. Solomos (Eds.), *Theories of race and racism*. Routledge.

Barth, F. (1969). *Ethnic groups and boundaries*. Routledge and Keegan Paul.

Barth, F. (1969). *Introduction to ethnic groups and boundaries*. Allen and Unwin.

Bauman, Z. (1990). Effacing the face: On the social management of moral proximity. *Theory, Culture and Society, 7*(1).

Belton, B. A. (2004). *Gypsy and traveller ethnicity: The social generation of an ethnic phenomenon*. Routledge.

Belton, B. A. (2005). *Questioning gypsy identity: Ethnic narratives in Britain and America*. AltaMira Press.

Boas, F. (1965). *The mind of primitive man*. Free Press.

Breakwell, G. M. (1992). *Social psychology of identity and the self concept*. Surrey University Press.

Butchart, A. (1998). *The anatomy of power: European constructions of the African body*. Zed Books.

Calhoun, C. (1994). *Social theory and the politics of identity*. Blackwell.

Castells, M. (1997). *The power of identity*. Blackwell.

Chapman, M. (Ed.). (1993). *Social and biological aspects of ethnicity*. Oxford University Press.

Clifford, J., & Marcus, G. E. (Eds.). (1986). *Writing culture*. University of California Press.

Clifford, J. (1988). *The predicament of culture*. Harvard University Press.

Coser, L. A. (Ed.). (1994). *On work, race and the sociological imagination*. University of Chicago Press.

Foucault, M. (1972). *The archaeology of knowledge*. Tavistock.

Geertz, C. (1973). *The interpretation of cultures*. Basic Books.

Gilroy, P. (1993). *The black atlantic*. Verso.

Goldberg, D. T. (1993). *Racist culture*. Blackwell.

Goldschmidt, W. (1992). *The human career*. Blackwell.

Gordon, C. (Ed.). (1980). *Power/Knowledge: Selected interviews and other writings 1972–1977 by Michael Foucault*. Pantheon.

Guibernau, M., & Rex, J. (Eds.). (1997). *The ethnicity reader*. Polity.

Hall, S. (1978). Racism and reation. In Commission for Racial Equality (Eds.), *Five views of multi-cultural Britain*. Commission for Racial Equality.

Hall, S. (1981a). *Cultural studies: Two paradigms*. In T. Bennett, et al. (Eds.), *Culture, ideology and social process*. Open University/Batsford.

Hall, S. (1981b). Teaching race. In A. James & Jeffcoate (Eds.), *The school in the multicultural society – a reader*. Harper & Row.

Hall, S. (1990). *Cultural identity and diaspora*. In J. Rutherford (Ed.), *Identitiy, community, culture and difference*. Lawrence and Wishart, first published in *Framework*, No. 36.

Hall, S. (1992, June 19). Our mongrel selves. *New Statesman and Society*, Suppl. pp. 6–8.

Hall, S. (1994). *Cultural identity and diaspora*. In P. Williams & L. Chrisman (Eds.), *Colonial discourse and postcolonial theory*. Routledge.

Hall, S. (1994). *The local and the global*. In King (Ed.), *Culture, globalisation and the world system*. Macmillian.

Hannaford, I. (1996). *Race: The history of an idea in the west*. John Hopkins University Press.

Henderson, H. (1992). *Alias MacAlias*. Polygon.

Hewitt, J. P. (1979). *Self and society* (2nd ed.). Allyn and Bacon.

Hobsbawn, E., & Ranger, T. (Eds.). (1983). *The invention of tradition*. Cambridge University Press.

Hughes, E. C. in Coser, L. A. (Ed.). (1994). *On work, race and the sociological imagination*. University of Chicago Press.

Jenkins, R. (1997). *Rethinking ethnicity*. Sage.

Jenkins, R. (1994). *Ethnic and racial studies*.

Jenkins, R. (1996). *Social identity*. Routledge.

Jones, S. (1993). *The language of the genes*. Flamingo.

Kohn, M. (1996). *The race gallery*. Vintage.

Kuper, A. (1983). *Anthropology and anthropologists: The modern British school*. Routledge.

Lieberman, L., Littlefield, A., & Reynolds, L. T. (1975). The debate over race thirty years and two centuries later. In Montague (Ed.), *Race and I.Q*. Oxford University Press.

McLoughlin, D. (1994). Nomadism in Irish travellers' identity. In M. McCann, S. O'Siochain, & J. Ruane (Eds.), *Irish travellers: culture and ethnicity*. Belfast: Institute of Irish Studies, The Queens University.

Malik, K. (1996). *The meaning of race*. Macillan.

Montagu, A. (1969). *The concept of race*. Collier-Macmillian.

Montagu, A. (1997). *Man's most dangerous myth. The fallacy of race*. Alta Mira.

Montagu, A. (Ed.). (1999). *Race & I.Q*. Oxford University Press.

Moore, H. L. (1994). *A passion for difference*. Polity.

Rex, J. (1986). *Race and ethnicity*. Open University Press.

Romanucci-Ross, L., & De Vos, G. (Eds.). (1995). *Ethnic identity*. Alta Mira.

Rutherford, J. (Ed.). (1990). *Identity: Community, culture, difference*. Lawrence and Wishart.

Rutherford, J. (1990). *Community, culture and difference*. Lawrence & Wishart.

Sampson, E. E. (1993). *Celebrating the other*. Harvester Wheatsheaf.

Sarup, M. (1996). *Identity, culture and the postmodern world*. Edinburgh University Press.

Scruton, R. (1990). In defence of the nation. In Clark (Ed.), *Ideas in politics in modern Britain*. MacMillian.

Smith, A. D. (1992). *Ethnic and racial studies*. Routledge.

Solomos, J., & Back, L. (1996). *Racism and society*. Macmillian.

Sollors, W. (Ed.). (1989). *The invention of ethnicity*. Oxford U.P.

Spicer, E. H. (1971). Persistent cultural systems. *Science, 174*(4011), 795–800.

Stepan, N. (1982). *The idea of race and science*. McMillian Press.

Turkle, S. (1995). *Life on the screen: Identity in the age of the Internet*. Simon and Schuster.

Weber, M. (1922). *Economy and society* (Vol. i). University of California Press.

Wirth, L. (1964). Urbanism as a way of life. In A. Riess (Ed)., *On cities and social life*. University of Chicago Press.

Woodward, K. (Ed.). (1997). *Identity and difference*. Sage.

Wray, M., & Newitz, A. (1997). *White Trash*. Routledge.

FREDERIC FROEBEL

Most teachers have little control over school policy or curriculum or choice of texts or special placement of students, but most have a great deal of autonomy inside the classroom. To a degree shared by only a few other occupations...public education rests precariously on the skill and virtue of the people at the bottom of the institutional pyramid.
                                                                    –Tracy Kidder

What follows looks at the influence and some of the ideas of Frederic Froebel. In the process I will be referring to some of his spiritual affinity to expand on his position. This does not look to promote any particular religious of spiritual 'way' or discipline and the reader might find that they will be able to transplant their own spiritual orientation within Frobel's language and direction.

Frederic Froebel was born in 1782, 36 years after Johann Heinrich Pestalozzi, another great innovator in education. He was one of the seminal thinkers who played a part in humanizing the educational process. Although setting most of his ideas in the context of the kindergarten, via his impact on under-five's education in Western Europe and America, his influence on schooling is hard to underestimate. Certainly his stance on the need for a sensitive and empathetic approach to learning encounters has provided generations of youth and play workers with inspiration and practice direction. The emphasis Froebel placed on play and enjoyment offers a means to take some of the sharp edges off didactic education across the broad spectrum of teaching and learning, an approach that has been vindicated time and again in practice.

It is probably not too much to claim that the informal influences in formal educational practice owe a great deal to the work and thought of Froebel. Indeed, those who are inclined to draw a heavy line between formal and informal education are probably doing Froebel and the many thousands of teachers and youth workers who have followed and developed his ideas, an injustice. Moreover, when one is able to observe outstanding examples of work with children and young people in what are often taken as purely informal contexts, it can be seen that the interplay between

B. Belton, *Developing Critical Youth Work Theory: Building Professional Judgment in the Community Context, 101–108.*

formality and informality is far more subtle than much of the literature on informal education suggests. From Froebel's perspective, the simplistic dichotomy often erected by writers who have attempted to generate the proposal of a separate realm of informal education undermines the essential organic wholeness of an authentically educational experience. Those working with children and young people, whether they are teachers or not, will, in terms of best practice, deploy both formal and informal methods and probably also, at points, inhabit that hinterland that exists between and around both. So, in practice, in the most nutritious educational encounters, there is no separation or difference – just a relatively seamless experience of learning.

Development of humanistic forms of education cannot be regarded as an invention on the part of anyone in particular, or the product of a certain moment in time. Indeed, the relatively aggressive notion of 'intervening' (a form of 'interference' or 'incursion') is redundant in Froebel's educational lexicon. Here, learning is a natural, organic and collaborative process, within which 'interference' is in fact an obstacle to understanding. The teacher and learner become interchangeable roles set in an association focused on the potential for cooperation.

Froebel's approach arose out of and was part of an historical and social moment and while attempts have been made to explain the formation and character of this phenomenon by referral to legislative activity and the insight of a few 'great men', such contentions are simplistic and not worthy in terms of explaining what was an exponential grow of spiritual, ethical and political awareness and practice. The work of individuals, discreet institutional incarnations and the enactment of educational and other legislation, do not of themselves explain the widespread undertaking that this educational bearing represents.

Although over the last quarter of a century, youth work and general professional practice involving children and young people outside school has continued to be welfare oriented it has, particularly in terms of initial training, been corralled into the educational fold. This is despite the fact that a parent is much more likely to ask a youth worker if their child is safe and having a good time than query the educational content of any given session. However most young people's experience of education is premised on the controlling character of school and how this infects the content and style of teaching, thus making the educational endeavour external to the learner. To a large extent, education (informal or formal) is experienced by most young people as something being done to, rather than by, them. Hence, even in the youth work realm wherein the 'autonomy' of the young person is seemingly given high regard as the 'voluntary' character of the practice, the main task of many youth workers is to somehow persuade, bribe, beg or even use low level threats to get young people to 'take responsibility for their own actions', for example, the withdrawal of potential rewards/privileges.

Within this sort of atmosphere the undertaking, say, of a day-trip with perhaps minimal participation of young people in the organizing process is often seen as a major victory and lauded as an example of 'good practice'.

The voluntarism doctrine is hung on to grimly in youth work when the reality for the young is that, if they need to mix socially in their 'free' time, they are usually faced with the fait accompli of entering pubs illegally, congregating in public spaces awaiting engagement with the police or accepting the facilities appointed for them to temporarily inhabit into which they are effectively herded. Would many of us, putting ourselves in the place of young people, from a critical education perspective, be likely to conclude that if this is voluntary then so were Bantustans?

'Inclusive' and 'participative' strategies are used across the horizon of youth education but they are deployed as a means to the same ends as more didactic methods. Forms of overt and perhaps more particularly covert control can quickly convert education into indoctrination or, in worse case scenarios, primal and unsophisticated forms of instruction or even propaganda. However, thinkers like Froebel represent a living strand of education that has understood that kindness and regard for the subject is much more efficient in terms of the collaborative pursuit of learning. It provides the justification for the development of a pact to indulge in an educational endeavour by learner and educator. Although this is nearly always unconscious and instinctive, at its most sophisticated, it can provide a situation wherein young people can be seen to follow a discernable theoretical and philosophical path that was established from the middle of the nineteenth century.

Froebel is important to youth work because he was one of the first people to develop a complete philosophy of humanist education practice that was underpinned by a basic principle - the assumption of 'dynamic growth'. For Froebel, the human infant responds to their environment from birth. He believed that meaning and purpose could be found in activity and that all human action stems from the inner reality of each person. As such, it is this 'inner reality' that the educator can usefully refer to in the promotion of action by the learner.

Our actions are, according to Froebel, the outward demonstration of a striving for what today we might think of as 'self-actualisation' or the effort to achieve ones potential. This represents our collective 'unity in God' in Froebel's words, the realization of which is the tendency of all living things to activate and, at the higher levels of consciousness, comprehend our essence. This was what Froebel thought of as the 'divine nature' of humanity, the spirit to be found in every person that entices them to extend their awareness of their nature. He saw this 'drive' as the 'divine' element played out in life and perhaps our project as educators. Acquisition of skills, forms of instruction and factual knowledge might be useful but these lie in the province of training. If we, as youth workers, are to set ourselves the task of playing a part in the education of others, working with people to move along the incline of 'insight' is required. It is this 'knowledge of self' that makes possible the generation of wisdom.

Froebel argues that is what education is (as opposed to forms of instruction or training) – the provision of attention to people's developing understanding, awareness and insight of themselves. This evolves to a second order when one begins to freely apply this wisdom (which is different to knowledge) to develop rationality i.e. the ability to think abstractly in an ordered and object-oriented manner. We are not just informed, our being is enhanced and our means of innovation and creativity is ignited. It is at this point that we discover, as Albert Einstein had it, that *imagination is more important than knowledge. Knowledge is limited. Imagination encircles the world.*

Our relationship to mind is felt as our consciousness of our intellect working is made manifest. This means of freedom and self awareness for Froebel gives rise to human happiness. What is liberated is 'the life of the mind'.

Froebel puts forward a number of forceful ideas to achieve this end. One of the most crucial is the effort to avoid making assumptions about people based on their superficial behaviour. He explains that what we perceive as 'good' behaviour may not necessarily be good and what we first understand to be 'bad' behaviour could well be the tangible signs of a struggle to behave admirably, a seeking for a way to behave well. What we see as unresponsive behaviour might be the outward expression of a person intensely following or wrestling with a line of thought or a set of ideas. Such consideration can be the motivation for us to reassess statements of the kind that propose someone 'lacks self-esteem' or that they are 'just seeking attention' and see them as more or less damaging accusations rather than the definite and, in some vague way, useful prognoses they may sometimes appear to be. Perhaps, we would also question the individuals whose qualifications to make such diagnoses are at least doubtful as are the means by which they might measure such indeterminable qualities like 'self-esteem'.

Froebel suggests that education must necessarily be permissive. The learner dictates the pace of what is to be encountered, explored, deconstructed, rationalized, deciphered and ultimately understood and how this is to be set within their intellect or otherwise deployed. The educator follows the learner, taking a stance that guards or protects rather than directs or interferes ('intervenes') with the process. Che Guevara suggested a similar response in his writings on guerrilla warfare, arguing that the guerrilla was doomed to fail if they entered a village with the idea of educating the people in that village. For Che the guerrilla first needs to seek education from the villagers about their position, perspectives and aspirations.

This idea logically follows on from Froebel's belief that good will come out of the essence of the person if this is a freely allowed expression. Unfortunately, too often we start from the negative assumption that the learner, given his or her head, will be destructive or disruptive and/or start out as ignorant (lacking that crucial divine essence). The presumption of the State, and/or its agencies, in sending 'educators' into a community, is that the targeted community has a lack of knowledge or awareness, which needs addressing. Why else task the educators with entering into the community in the first place?

The shift that both Froebel and Guevara ask of us is quite daunting in that it goes against many of the basic assumptions about those we work with. We enter the community as learners to be educated in order that we might be involved in a process of growth. We acknowledge that divine essence but in doing so probably give up control of what the learning might be or where it might lead. The questions it might be caused to be asked may be exciting but with excitement there is risk – this is no 'safe' environment.

What is it that the youth worker as a community educator might want to educate people in? What sort of 'school' is to be initiated? People rarely ask for a community educator to come into their lives – youth workers often just 'turn up' on the strength of a successful funding bid or the 'concerns' of people with little or no contact with the 'targeted groups'. Froebel argues that the person will in fact seek what is best for them, that which is appropriate to their needs. He makes the point that plants and animals given space, time, rest and protection from violent intervention are likely to flourish much more than if they are cramped, rushed, worked hard and interfered with. He asserts that humans are too often regarded as no more than pieces of wax or clay, to be moulded into a chosen shape (this is perhaps the essence of competency-based, curriculum-led ideas that place high priority on accreditation). For Froebel, this can result in people being forced into purposes unsuited to their nature, which might be experienced and reacted to as little more than a form of colonization. Even reading and writing might come into this category. As a dyslexic, I can say that I only came to literacy when I was ready not at the behest of some teacher or even community educator.

Following on from this, Froebel suggests that teaching, to be effective, needs to move away from prescribing or determining what people should do. It is interesting to look at how many times books focusing on informal education use the words 'should' and 'must'. This kind of attitude impedes and destroys that essence Froebel refers to. He argues that it is rare to see an 'unspoilt' human, someone who has not been hurt or scared by what amounts to efforts to deter them from achieving their unique potential, the pathway of their essence. He asks, 'How can we know when a mind has been harmed'. This provokes all sorts of subsidiary questions. It makes it hard for us to have any definite faith in the depictions of people as having 'special needs' or lacking 'self-esteem'. These are, after all, nearly always, labels applied by professionals, rather than conditions adopted by individuals.

What Froebel is saying is that we need to question the assumption of deficit. As R.D. Laing constantly asked by way of his work, he is pleading with us to see behaviour as, usually, a perfectly explicable response to conditions – a way of seeking to express the positive life of the mind, our inner reality, our positively charged essence.

This does not mean that he wants us to accept behaviour that is dangerous or damaging to others. It is perhaps part of the role of the educator to work with the learner (and remember these roles are interchangeable) to reveal what behaviour or aspects of the learner's behaviour might be troublesome. We enter into a concerted transaction, the object of which is to demonstrate the effects and consequences of behaviour and, from Froebel's point of view, follow the example of Christ and impose no external standards.

The educator can provide an ideal or an example of the self active, self reliant individual. This, for Froebel, is the point of education. It exists to call forth freedom and an associated ability to be self determining within a collaborative spirit. The alternative is to educate (train, instruct, indoc-trinate) people (via propaganda) to be tyrants or dependents. For him, most education in the contemporary period would be about demonstrating authority relations – I, the teacher, am stronger and have more authority than you, the pupil/student. As such I will impose my will and standards on you – Might is right! The bully is vindicated. It has to be said that the teacher does have authority but so does the student or pupil. The tragedy is that the former is so often 'over realized' at the expense of the latter.

The educator, in order to be regarded as an educator, is 'two sided'. S/he gives and takes, unites and divides, orders and follows, is active and passive, decisive and permissive, firm and flexible. But the learner, in the best of situations, also needs to be as accommodating. If this is allowed to occur, if the 'educational association' is not based on the arbitrary expression of authority, the idea of 'right' emerges between the learner and the educator as their roles interact, are exchanged and entwine.

Act and see what follows from your action. This is the basis of rationality and science and it is the foundation of Froebel's philosophy. It is this process that makes the internal external and the external internal. The more practiced one becomes at this interplay between self and the world, the more one is able to think abstractly, the more ideas can enter the realm of reality and the more reality can accommodate ideas.

Education, being the product of our divine essence, can thus be understood as the cultivation of the divine nature of human beings. For Froebel, it is indicative of our unity in God. We create environments wherein people may depict, through the living out of their lives, what is infinite and eternal. As such, every child, every person not only 'matters', they are indispensable. They are educators and learners and part of the education and learning of others. They are essential (of their essence) to the human race. Thus it is harmful to regard development and education as static or isolated processes. The child is not just imitative for if we were just this we would amount to no more than lifeless copies of other things. We have a creative and expressive essence and this is stifled by one dimensional 'educational' practices.

For Froebel, every person, to realize their selfhood, requires the freedom to express their unique potential. This is what we, as youth workers seek to provide. For Froebel, God is mirrored in infinite difference. The project to create sameness or regimentation is antithetical to that which Froebel takes to be the realisation of our essence, the spirit of God. He tries to show us that we are set in a universal pattern and that there is no need to hurry to reach some externally defined standard or stage of development. He wants us to regard ourselves as the creative source of authority, what Henry Handel Richardson saw as 'the getting of wisdom'. Life then becomes oceanic. It has no sharp divisions between stages, our existence can be understood in its orgasmic and organic sense. The unreal, notional dichotomies between child, adolescent and adult, black and white, male and female, formal and informal are transcended. Our work and all work then becomes creative. Collectively and in connection we move towards creativity.

To create such a path we need to move away from hindering progress by making it our primary purpose to be 'helpful' or 'supportive'. This approach sees people as somehow 'helpless' and unable to support themselves and as such pitiful. This deficit connection is, in reality, interference. Such activity has material ends and is not centred on spiritual development. It sees the person as limited in what they can do and restricts what they might do. We can 'help' we can 'support', but we can also take help from those we work with and accept their support. In truth, isn't it we, in our work with others, who need them to support and help us? We need them because they define our work and without them we would have no work to do. Credit where credit's due!

The test of a good teacher is not how many questions she can ask her pupils that they will answer readily, but how many questions she inspires them to ask her which she finds it hard to answer – Alice Wellington Rollins

BIBLIOGRAPHY

Ackland, M. (2005). *Henry handel richardson*. Cambridge University Press.
Courthope Bowen, H. (1968). *Froebel and education by self activity*. C Chivers.
Guevara, E. (1961). *Guerrilla warfare*. M R Press.
Handel Richardson, H. (2007). *The getting of wisdom*. The Echo Library.
Heafford, M. (1967). *Pestalozzi: His thought and its relevance today*. Methuen.
Laing, R. D. (1970). *Sanity, madness and the family*. Pelican.
Laing, R. D. (1970). *The divided self*. Pelican.
Laing, R. D. (1971). *Self and others*. Pelican.
Liebschner, J. (2006). *A child's work: Freedom and guidance in Froebel's educational theory and practice*. Lutterworth Press.
Wild, S. (2000). *Raising curious, creative, confident kids: The Pestalozzi experiment in child-based education*. Shambhala Publications Inc.
The Getting of Wisdom. (1977). Directed by Bruce Beresford, screenplay Eleanor Witcombe.

INFORMAL EDUCATORS OR BUREAUCRATS AND SPIES? DETACHED YOUTH WORK AND THE SURVEILLANCE STATE

The Matrix is a system…when you're inside, you look around, what do you see? Businessmen, teachers, lawyers, carpenters. The very minds of the people we are trying to save. But until we do, these people are still a part of that system…You have to understand, most of these people are not ready to be unplugged. And many of them are so inured, so hopelessly dependent on the system, that they will fight to protect. Morpheus, in Andy and Larry Wachowski's (1999) *The Matrix*

The following has been adapted from a talk given to the Federation for Detached Youth Work Conference by Detached Youth Worker Tania de St Croix on 13th November 2008 (Young people's names have been changed).

Tania has been involved in youth work, play schemes and community activism since leaving school in 1993. She grew up in Bath and has mostly lived and worked there and in Manchester. She is currently a detached youth worker for a small charity in Hackney, London.

Last week, Patricia said to me: *'NOT ANOTHER BLOODY FORM!'* Patricia is 13, bright, enthusiastic, fun, and she has had enough of filling in forms. For every project she gets involved in, there seems to be another one. Patricia says,

> *'If my mum didn't want me to come on the trip why would she let me out the house?'*

The only times Patricia argues with me are over these forms.

When they don't want to do something, the young people I work with use an expression: *It's long.* That means, 'It will take a long time' and as such will be boring. They mean 'It's not worth the bother'.

According to Patricia, *'The forms are LONG!'* and she says that they are the only thing she really dislikes about our project. You might agree with her, a lot of other young people certainly do. But you may be thinking, 'It's

B. Belton, *Developing Critical Youth Work Theory: Building Professional Judgment in the Community Context, 109–118.*

our job to persuade young people to do things they don't want to do at times – to change 'it's long' into 'I can do this'.'

I wouldn't disagree with that if I believed that was in the young people's best interests. But I don't believe all this form filling is altogether useful to them and this is the main reason I have written what follows. I'm not a manager nor am I a policy maker, I'm a face-to-face detached youth worker, but like Patricia, I have had enough!

The huge increase of bureaucracy in youth work I believe is to the detriment of young people. It is harmful in terms of our relationships with them, and it is the antithesis of what makes detached youth work effective.

I am committed to the practice of detached youth work and for most of the time find it a fulfilling and stimulating profession. I don't like to think of myself as a bureaucrat although my job includes data input, counting young people and their so-called outcomes. I'm pretty sure that few youth workers on entering practice see a big part of their role as being 'information management' and identifying 'performance indicators' but in actuality such tasks are hard to avoid.

And the information we supposedly need is increasing. Just for starters, the need for full names, addresses, dates of birth, postcodes is not even questioned. I have been involved with a couple of projects recently that required this information about a young person in order for that individual to be seen as involved in our practice. No matter how much they might be taking part in or be the focus of youth work officially, until this data is collected and processed, nothing has taken place. This madness hasn't always been the way of things. In my first detached youth work post I was in contact with or recognised around 100 young people but I hardly knew any of their surnames, let alone their postcodes.

Slowly it started to change. My next post in detached youth work included organising a plethora of day-trips, residential events and exchanges. Trips required consent forms and that seemed fair enough. The forms would be taken on the trip with us and when we got back they were filed away or stuffed in a box somewhere. I was not required to transfer this information onto a database and if such an idea had been mooted I would have been surprised and uncomfortable. If I had been asked to share the information with others, I would have quickly and certainly said 'NO'.

The last summer in that job was five years ago, and I got a taste of things to come. I had gained funding from one of those government schemes for year 11 leavers and suddenly I had to ask the young people to complete detailed, and what I (and they) saw as intrusive, questionnaires that sought information such as if they had used drugs, committed a crime and asked about their family's financial situation. Billy, a 16 year old, said to me,

'This is a really nosey form. Why do they need to know all this?' A good question – nowhere on the questionnaire was this adequately explained. I told him that, as far as I was concerned, it was his choice whether or not to answer the questions. *You can fill them in or we can screw up the forms and look for money elsewhere. I don't mind what you decide, the forms really are nosey.* But Billy said, *'No. The Lake District trip's next week – we need that money'.* And he persuaded the rest of the group to fill in the forms.

But what choice did those young people really have – cancel their summer holiday and most likely get their youth worker in trouble, or just fill in the bloody form?

This led me to believe that we have got into a position where most of us employed in youth work are obliged to be part of an elaborate spying operation focusing on the behaviour and life-style of the young people we work with. We collect and effectively collate this 'intelligence' on behalf of central or local government, just to keep our projects going. This applies as much to the voluntary sector as it does the statutory services as both draw down funding that comes directly or indirectly from the State under every conceivable guise from the Youth Media Fund to grants via the Youth Justice Board. Recently the Audit Commission said that youth workers could spend up to a third of their time trying to secure funding from any one of seven government departments and they all require 'information'.

It might sound drastic to call our activities, that are either implicit in our job descriptions or part of funding packages, 'spying', but that's what it amounts to. The young people I work with would probably call it 'grassing' or 'snitching'. Confidentiality seems to have gone out of fashion and covert use of information taken its place. Many of us now use local government or Connexions databases, directly or through our funders. These databases are seen by thousands of people who all have the authority to access information about a young person and what services they are using on any given day over any particular period. How can this be anything but a definite breach of the privacy of young people and their families? A mum can't look and see if her daughter attended a dance project last night but professional strangers can.

This incursion will be extended when the national Contact Point database starts. It is intended to include every single child in the UK, their name, address, gender, date of birth, parents, names of GPs and other professionals who have contact with them. It will not be possible to opt out of this hugely invasive prying into community life. At least 330,000 people will have access to this database, including some of us youth workers. The database has experienced a few technical hitches, but at the time of writing, it is due to start in a few months time. These databases are just part of the wider surveillance culture that will allow the State to observe and record patterns of personal behaviour and social activity that will facilitate the prediction of individual, group and community conduct the point of which is control.

Before all this has got underway, right now there are huge amounts of information collected about children and young people and all of it can be accessed by the police and much of it by other professional interest groups. For example:

- Over half a million children and young people are on the national DNA database. Most of these individuals have not been convicted of any crime.
- Young people in London get free bus travel but in exchange they carry an electronic photo card that records every journey they make.
- Schools have started to collect pupils' fingerprints ostensibly for library and canteen use.
- Some youth clubs issue ID cards with barcodes to record young people's 'participation'.
- A number of detached youth workers have even been asked to carry barcode scanners with them on the streets to identify the young people they are working with.

Youth workers have traditionally sought to work in the interests of young people. We have not seen ourselves as 'cuddle police' or allies of the very adult authority that many of those we work with seek to at least temporarily escape from. This might have been idealistic but what is wrong with idealism? For all this, perhaps we need to be looking at ways of raising general awareness of this attack on not only the privacy of young people but, along with the mass activation of CCTV, an incursion into the intimate lives of families and communities. If we are to be advocates, working with and for young people, standing alongside the communities they inhabit and are part of in defence of human rights and civil liberties, how can we just be meekly complicit with this intrusion? Why do we not simply refuse to take an active part in these insidious and offensive surveillance systems?

As things stand, we are in effect coercing young people to supply us with information about themselves which we pass on to others. If the young people get a choice at all it is often mediated by subtle (or blatant) bribery, such as access to free or cheap resources, with prizes, incentives or barely disguised threats to lose holidays or facilities. Just as often we are using our relationships with them as a means to fulfil organisational goals. For example, one of my youth service colleagues was given a five page form that he was meant to get young people to fill in on the streets. He had been told by his new boss that he needed to get this done. Somehow the worker persuaded a few young people to do it. They did it because of his good relationship with them. But I would argue that he was at the same time undermining or even cheapening this relationship. How is it we can coarsely 'use relationships' in this way? How is this in any way ethical? This is not blaming my colleague as he was stranded between the proverbial rock and a hard place.

To some young people it is starting to seem normal that youth workers want all this information about them. Like Patricia, they might object but they have never known any different. We are close to being seen as synonymous with our intelligence gathering task rather than being identified as the allies of young people we once were.

Over the years, youth workers have stopped offering confidentiality with regard to young people's personal details and information. Our confidentiality or so-called 'data protection' statements now include so many get-out clauses that they are almost worthless. We can no longer be trusted and as such we probably need to ask ourselves some serious questions:

– Do we tell young people where their information goes, how it might be used and who might see it?
– Do we tell them if we record our contact with them every time we meet them?
– Are we hiding the truth (lying)?
– Do we even know ourselves what happens to this 'intelligence'? If not, are we happier not knowing (being ignorant)?
– Other questions have occurred to me:
– What about a family who have run away from domestic violence and made a new life – what happens to their safety if their address can be located on a database?
– What about families on the Witness Protection Scheme?
– What about the large number of us who have a healthy mistrust of authorities and their capacity to keep us and information about us safe?

I am most worried by the youth services which have streamlined their systems. I have a couple of examples. Kent is implementing youth club membership cards with barcodes. As their website says,

It saves time instead of using a manual system and the information obtained is used to produce statistics that the government need about young people.

No mention is made of what happens if the young people refuse to get a membership card. Would they still be allowed to use the youth centre? If they were, how would this be commensurate with equality of opportunity?

In Weston Super Mare is the Barcode café youth centre, – I hoped at first that this was tongue-in-cheek but unfortunately the name was eponymous. If you are a young person in Weston Super Mare, to use this youth cafe and to get discounts on other facilities, you need a barcoded key (to be 'barcoded'). Personal information, apparently,

...will not be disclosed to anyone outside the council

I suppose that's meant to reassure but how can this be guaranteed and who exactly is 'inside' the council? Perhaps other café names might be 'Sneaky's', 'The Interrogation Joint' or the 'Surveillance, Nosiness, Observation Overview Place (SNOOPs)?

It is difficult for a young person to refuse to fill in a form when asked by their youth worker, especially if it means they won't be allowed to take part in an activity that their friends and maybe even family are involved with as a result. But many of the young people I work with do refuse which shows how strongly they feel.

For example, John is about 15, quite small, articulate and intelligent. He doesn't go to school. He has an easy smile and a quick temper or is passionate (depending on your perspective). It was weeks before he talked to me and months before he was what you might call friendly. He got involved in our film project and his acting was fantastic. We asked him for parental consent to appear on the finished film but he absolutely refused to take the form home or to fill it in himself. We said that it was a legal requirement and he said he'd rather not be in the film than fill in the form. He said, 'I don't trust people'.

We risked it and made him a special form just requiring his own signature and no other details. So he was happy, and he had a starring role in the film. One day on the street John gave my colleague his mobile number, out of the blue and without being asked. It was like getting a present. That was an important gift of acceptance and trust. Over time, John has told us his surname and his home address. I don't ask him anything outright. I let him tell me what he wants to tell me. I would never put his details on a database because I know how strongly he feels. As such I don't really 'intervene' with him but make the room for him to interact with me. Evidence has shown that John doesn't like being intervened with – why should he? Intervention means 'interference' or 'intrusion' – that is what it is.

There are many people that I work with who feel much the same as John. I react to them in approximately the same way as I did to John. These relationships are fragile and precious and can only survive with the kind of fair mutuality that John demanded.

If I am honest, to make up for those who don't give anything away, I collect the details of those who don't protest, the ones who want to be helpful, who give their details because they trust us or simply wish to cooperate. These are the young people who fill out the Youth Opportunity Fund forms, those I refer to other organisations for so-called 'support'. They're all going to have their details put on databases and it will partly because of my actions. As such as much as we work with them they are working with us – we rely on their help, their support or sympathy for our plight.

I am an optimist. I don't want to be negative because I continue to believe in, am committed to and find fulfilment in detached youth work. It's a privilege to have an insight into young people's worlds, to be included in some of their conversations, to do things together, to debate and discuss with them and in the best of all possible worlds be included in their development and dialectic.

But parts of my work are soul destroying because they get in the way of what made detached youth work special. Two major issues arise here, issues for everyone who works with young people.

The first big issue is the growing surveillance culture and its impact on young people, and considerations of equality, choice, privacy and justice.

The second issue is particularly important for those of us working on the streets. By using all these forms and databases and information sharing systems, we potentially destroy our privileged association with young people. Calling the street 'young people's territory' is a misnomer as young people on the street are always someone's responsibility – the police, their parents, social services etc and they are subject to laws including that of trespass, dispersal orders and many aspects of the Criminal Justice Act. The fact is that youth clubs and centres are much more 'their territory' in terms of legality and responsibility than the street. However, despite this incongruity, our relationships with those we work with, for and among needs to be negotiated on their terms because the only concrete resource a detached youth worker has with a young person is that potential relationship. In short, for the work to happen the relationship has to be made. If this 'making' is compromised by attempting to inculcate a surveillance culture into our approach then the whole role is, probably irretrievably, undermined.

WHAT CAN WE DO ABOUT THIS?

It's quite scary even thinking about opposing the surveillance culture as it is State sponsored and serviced. Those with authority over the construction of this nexus have been clever because in many cases if we don't send in the forms or we refuse to fill in the databases we will lose resources for our projects and potentially our jobs will be threatened. Or at least that is what we have been inclined to believe.

In addition, and this really makes me angry, if we even speak out against these surveillance systems we are accused of not caring about abused children.

Recently, I attended a training course on the Common Assessment Framework. Whenever anyone questioned the invasion of privacy this might represent or other potential problems the trainer asked something like, 'You don't want to see another Victoria Climbie case do you?' Such a question invites only a yes or no answer and either way you lose. This was using fear to silence opposition.

However, it is not a given that computerised information sharing will save lives nor is it likely that it would have saved Victoria Climbie. But by invoking extremely sad and rare cases, those pushing for more information sharing make it very difficult for individuals to voice our opposition. The culture of surveillance is premised on a culture of fear.

Firstly, to manage this fear it is clear that we would need to address our isolation. Working in partnership with others could be our strongest defence against the success of the most intrusive information sharing. We can make allies wherever we can – within youth work, with others who work with young people and with campaigning organisations such as Liberty and No 2 ID.

Secondly, it makes sense to work with and alongside young people. This would be a valuable addition to our work as ethical practitioners and the means to the political and social education of those who are at the centre of our work. We can ask young people for their views, opinions and feelings on these issues. And then, most importantly, they and us can together act on our findings (counter intelligence?).

Thirdly, we can speak up in meetings and training sessions, despite any silencing tactics.

Lastly, what would happen if we got together and boycotted these databases or we refused to supply information about individuals unless it was a matter of life and death? Why can we not repudiate any suggestion of working in partnership with organisations who abuse personal information?

Perhaps if we took these types of action as individuals it might not be long before we lost our funding or our job or both (the two often go together of course). However, if we all did it, workers backed by young people, while we might not put an end to surveillance culture, it would act as an authoritative example to those we work with that there are a few more options beyond mere acquiescence – we would no longer be role models in promotion of fear tactics. It might also loosen up information supplied to young people about how information about them might potentially be used. This opens up all sorts of tactical and strategic options for them and their communities that are as numerous as the bounds of our collective imaginations.

This might also demonstrate to young people that we are on their side and show our managers that we will not easily be persuaded or cajoled into spying on young people. Our trade unions can be proactive on these issues if we 'help' them to be and I believe that this is the kind of industrial action that nearly everybody would support, young people and their parents most of all. But the time for action is always, always 'Right Now' and we can start to think about practical opposition for ourselves from this moment and swiftly turn thought into action – reflection has its limits.

Perhaps it is helpful to revisit the core aspects and values of detached youth work. We are youth workers and as such have a heritage of concern for the welfare and care of those we work with, for and among. Our history as a profession has been concerned with promoting the taking of responsibility, dealing with consequences and the faith that communities have it within them to act in their own interests. So issues of rights and privacy are considerations we should have every expectation of ourselves to work on with individuals and communities.

What right do we have to go and ask those we work with for personal information? As detached workers we have established that our role is premised on dealing with young people on their terms but on whose terms and to whom are we acting as a conduit of intelligence?

Is it not time to stop before we are seen by young people not just as victims who need their help with managing the surveillance culture by sacrificing their privacy but a willing part of that culture?

We can work in young people's interests. We can take action and speak out where-ever we can and stay true to our creed as youth workers before selling our souls to become the bureaucrats, servants of and spies for surveillance culture. But the biggest word in all this is '**we**'.

Let me tell you why you're here. You're here because you know something. What you know you can't explain, but you feel it. You've felt it your entire life, that there's something wrong with the world. You don't know what it is, but it's there, like a splinter in your mind, driving you mad. It is this feeling that has brought you to me.

Do you know what I'm talking about? Morpheus, in Andy and Larry Wachowski's (1999) *The Matrix*

BIBLIOGRAPHY

Davis, A. (2003). *Are prisons obsolete?* Seven Stories Press.
Foucault, M. (1977). *Discipline and punish: Birth of the prison.* Viking.
Garfinkel, S. (2000). *Database nation: The death of privacy in the 21st century.* O'Reilly Media, Inc.

CHAPTER 9

SWIMMING AGAINST THE TIDE?

*It's how we spend our time here and now, that really matters. If you
are fed up with the way you have come to interact with time, change it.*
– Marcia Wieder

This chapter has been included to demonstrate how community based
workers are being increasingly deployed as an adjunct to the growing
surveillance culture focused on youth. At the same time, it records how
youth workers feel this role to be quite alien to their practice, morality and
sense of professional ethics.

The motivation for what follows comes from the experience and insight
of Tania de St Croix who collected the responses included in this chapter
from a workshop that followed the talk detailed in the previous chapter.

At the workshop Tania asked participants to share their experiences of
tracking and monitoring young people and how this affected their work. of
the 20 participants, all were either detached youth workers or detached
youth work managers. Most were from the statutory sector and a few from
the voluntary sector. These individuals worked in a variety of settings, both
rural and urban. Four participants had experience of different legal and
policy frameworks regarding monitoring and information sharing, two of
them in Wales, one in Scotland, and one in Sweden. The workshop was
recorded and transcribed with the permission of the participants.

The participants were familiar with a range of information sharing
systems. Most were employed by youth services which had purchased
database systems from private companies including Electronic Youth
Services, Youthbase, and QES. Some used database systems which were
part of wider local authority, education or Connexions systems. Other
services and voluntary organisations deployed internal databases. In
addition, most of the workshop participants had been requested or required
to give young people's personal information to funding bodies including
PAYP (Positive Activities for Young People), the police, drug action teams
and Primary Care Trusts. Some had used the Common Assessment
Framework (CAF) format which brought forward the comment from one
workshop participant, 'If there is an intrusive form then that is it'. The

*B. Belton, Developing Critical Youth Work Theory: Building Professional Judgment
in the Community Context, 119–130.*

national children's database Contact Point was discussed only briefly as nobody at the workshop had any experience of it.

The purpose of this chapter is to provide a space for the voices of youth workers who, for a variety of reasons, question data sharing systems. They represent and give a voice to a growing feeling within the profession.

DETACHED YOUTH WORKERS' VIEWS ON INFORMATION SHARING

Most of the workshop participants had serious objections to detached youth workers being involved in tracking young people, although the issue of whether young people should be tracked at all was not the focus of the workshop.

A key objection to the databases and information sharing systems was that they were seen to infringe on young people's privacy as well as the confidentiality between the youth worker and young people. Some responses around these issues were

I think a lot of the information gathered on young people now is intrusive and it is asking questions that really I wonder why they are being asked in the first place.

The worst thing about it is we have to ask the young people what their sexuality is. You're thinking, 'why does it matter?' It's got nothing to do with their sexuality. That's the thing... especially because [in my voluntary agency] we're not in a position to help those young people if they're in a place where they're not sure and they want to talk about it with someone.

I can access pretty much every single young person in our authority and that doesn't necessarily sit very well with me. You can imagine, if I'm a parent, I happen to be a youth worker, I want to know what my son or daughter was doing last night, I just look. 'Click!' Nobody stops me for doing it, not a single person! They might say it's confidential. Bollocks!

Part of me sees the benefit of it but one issue I have is the names. Why do we need to put names of young people onto a database on the internet which they say is secure? Sorry, but I don't believe anything on a computer is secure at all.

Many of the workshop participants were concerned that young people were not being informed about the collection and sharing of their personal information.

A lot of the forms that I see that young people's data goes on have got nothing with regard to data protection. Do they know it's going to be held on a database and can be used by other agencies?

A young person came in and saw the QES system we've got and saw her name on it and I asked, 'Did you know your name was on there?' She replied, 'No'.

'What do you think about that?' I asked and she said, 'I don't know really'. This young person didn't know it was going onto a database and was really unsure about all this information being contained about her.

You're asking people for consent to attend a trip and then you're using that information to go onto a database that they've not consented to.

The only evidence we have in our area of how data is used, it's used against the young people who are judged to be a threat or a risk to society... When I've raised the issue, do these young people know that you're discussing this, you've got this information, etc., etc., I haven't been invited back any more. Surely that's wrong.

A significant number of participants had experienced the use of youth project membership cards in their areas. These often included barcodes or identity numbers which linked holders to information gathering systems.

We have a database within our voluntary service ... and they've just mentioned about having I.D. cards, and they've put it to the young people as, 'So then it's easier for you to sign in and out, easy come, easy go', and they're like, 'Oh yeah, it's a bit of responsibility, you have a card', and that's how it's sold to the young people, and they're just kind of like, 'Yeah, wicked, I've got a card', and they don't really think of the thought process behind it, its almost a tracking device on them.

My concerns are about membership forms. When young people fill in membership forms, sometimes they want to do it, sometimes they don't, and then I was told if they do not fill in the membership form they cannot access the youth provision. But as far as I'm concerned whether they fill it in or not they access the youth provision because they leave their house to socialise and come and partake of activities.

It's like that whole thing of customers, seeing young people as consumers of the future. Young people are into this type of drug or having this kind of sex. I think it's a bit sinister that the people running this are people like Capita [an organisation that describes

121

itself as delivering '…its market leading outsourcing services from more than 300 sites, including over 50 specialist business centres of service excellence'].

We've just started creating a membership card and it's the same type of thing, you're like bribing them, you say, you get a free membership card, but why would they want to pay for one anyway?

There was that whole thing with the Connexions Card where it was like they would be able to get discounts and vouchers but only in selected stores and oddly no independent suppliers.

Many participants agreed that some young people do not get the support they need from a range of professionals and some felt a shared database could help address this.

It can be useful because at the moment I'm trying to work with a young lad who I don't know any information about and at the moment I've got to use my car, walk, meet the professionals one at a time. It would be so nice just to look at what's happened and then I can make an informed decision, do I then need to work further with him?

However, many participants who already used the new systems had not experienced greater support for young people. The first quotation is from somebody using a system shared with schools in his area.

No one's contacted me, and I know a lot of the young people I work with haven't been going to school or have been excluded from school. It marks up a question mark- if we've got the system in place to benefit young people, why in the past 12 months hasn't that happened?

There are loads of multi-agency panels where everyone will have a long chat about the young people but there's no one to do the work with them. There's so many people chatting, recording, tracking, monitoring, but no one's actually building relationships, getting to know them, caring about them, showing them any compassion, respect, engagement.

It seems like there's a lot of information we're being asked to give. It's being collated, someone's got statistics but what are they doing about it? Nothing is being done with this information.

With the information sharing thing I think that it's ok if it's for the interests of the young person and they're going to get something out of it. I'm just not convinced giving all this information on young people is for their benefit. I think it's going to be used for the wrong reasons.

We've got a thing with the police at the moment where they're meant to share information with us and we're meant to share information with them. Like say something's gone on in your area, you need to know really if you're going out on the street if there's been a massive fight or something and it could be a safety issue. But in reality the police don't inform you. They want to know things from you but they don't tell you anything.

The slight difference on those CAF forms is they're asking professionals to make value judgements, so it's sort of, 'in your opinion what are their social skills?' ... You really start to see the bias of certain professionals about people's lives and lifestyles.

There's so much tracking and monitoring, but I'm not seeing any improvement in services. There's so many young people who cannot access services, services are not available for them...Social services: over-run. Youth service: under-funded. We're doing all this tracking and monitoring but is it making any difference?... In fact there's a reduction in money, core funding. All I know is the systems keep going down, the tracking keeps happening, but nothing is getting better.

Some participants expressed mixed feelings about the information sharing aspects of their role.

I'm sorry but I'm an informal educator, a bureaucrat and a spy, and I'm sat here and my head's buzzing because we have a system that up until 20 minutes ago I thought was a really positive system... I also have to work with young people and say to them, 'Ok you're not telling me this detail but how come then I can go onto Facebook and you've got every single thing about yourself? You're stood there with really provocative poses...' I'm really sitting on the fence and I need to see both sides because for me to do work, to manage workers, to support young people, I have to move right through this whole thing. By the time I have a young person who wants to be in employment, who wants to access services, they'll have to give that information.

The main issues for me at the moment are to do with getting my staff to fill in forms that I don't really believe in myself and knowing that I'm going to get into trouble if I don't get them to do it, and trying to convince my staff when they know really that I don't believe in these forms... staff are feeling very, very uncomfortable with doing that and not wanting to do it and resisting doing it, and me obviously having to be the person in the middle who is getting them to do it when I don't really believe in it myself. So, I'm wrestling with that inner conflict in myself really.

EFFECTS ON DETACHED YOUTH WORK

Many participants felt that information gathering demands caused a conflict with their ability to build relationships with marginalised young people.

I would not feel comfortable taking names because it deters from the interaction with the young people... it's a bit intrusive... I talk to some young people two or three times, you just get into a general conversation and it's maybe the third or fourth time before you ask, what's your name?

Where's the relationship building part of it? That's what I've said to my team, is build up the relationship. If a young person then on your session wants to give a name, they give a name. When you take them out on an activity that's the point where you know who you're dealing with, they are quite accepting then to fill out the form to say, 'it's safe with my mum, my mum's told me that it''s safe to go', you get everything then.

The young people, especially I find the ones that are normally in trouble with other people, they are always like, 'What are you going to do with my contact details, what are you going to do with my name?' "

I know some of our workers, they don't want to read what other workers think the young person is like, because when you meet a young person, we talked about the ethos being about withholding judgement... how can you do that when you know how many times they've been excluded... all that kind of thing. If in the back of your mind you know they've back-chatted teachers, you may approach them slightly differently.

Some detached youth workers who had been gathering personal details for some time felt that young people were getting used to it, perhaps accepting the new systems uncritically. It was not clear whether all the young people had eventually accepted the system or if the workers had lost contact with those who were more critical.

They see all the benefits, the membership card and vouchers that we offer them, but they don't see the deeper side of it of all the information they're giving and where it's going to end up.

In the past 12 months young people have got quite used to it, so often they say, 'Oh do you want me to put my name on the sheet?' and they're ok with it.

At the moment we take signing in sheets out with us every session, which the young people happily fill in really. They don't know. Sometimes they say, 'Where's it going?' but they don't know. Some of them are as young as 13 so when they see the older ones filling in the sheet they're happy to write down their names. In tiny print at the bottom it does say, 'Your information will go on a database'. Whether they actually know what a database is, is a different matter... Well, I don't know where it goes... I just don't know.

As well as affecting face-to-face work with young people, data collection systems also affected detached youth workers' evaluation and planning.

There's an issue in that it's a bit of a solo task feeding in to a database. We went to a meeting a couple of months ago when one of our service managers said, 'We don't need any paper anymore, we don't need to do those recording sheets, just feed it in to the computer, it's all on there', and for me I think it's a real concern because, certainly for detached youth workers, at the end of the session we usually debrief on the streets or in a cafe, and for me that dynamic between workers reflecting on their work and discussing what they're doing and why they're doing it and analysing it is really key; it's not just about numbers and ethnicity and age, it's actually about, 'How am I co-working?' and my concern at the moment is not to lose that opportunity of discussing and improving the co-work relationship which is central for detached work.

If you've got a target set, you're working to achieve that target. That's what I feel. I am working just to achieve those targets in my authority. That's what I've got to do. Once I've achieved them, fantastic, I'm happy then, I can have an easy life for the rest of the year. Then the next year starts and I do it again.

For some, the administrative burden of data sharing systems detracted from the skilled interpersonal aspects of youth work.

I've got to enter details and I call myself a very well paid admin worker, that's my new title for myself, because I just spend a lot of my time entering data into a computer. I didn't train and go to college and everything to spend my time entering data from an evaluation sheet into a computer database, I just spend hours doing it! I just think it's boring, a total waste of my time and individual resources doing it.

The more experienced senior workers who hopefully would have some more skills and knowledge and ability are all putting rubbish into computers so no one's actually doing high quality youth work with very complex needs from young people. I really believe this whole data collection business is knocking out the quality of the work.

I'm not that sort of person. I can't, I hate putting data into a computer. I get about ten minutes and then it breaks down and I get annoyed, frustrated with it and I hit the computer and I swear lots. And it's like, why can't this work, why can't this be easy? Simple? But it's the way we're going and we've got to do it.

PRESSURE TO CONFORM

Participants felt under direct and indirect pressure to take part in systems that share personal information about young people. As young people are tracked so are those who work with them.

I think we all are under pressure to collate and to collect information on young people.

I get told, 'targets, targets, targets' continuously, I go into my workplace and I'm told, 'have you met your contacts, have you met your recorded outcomes, have you met your accredited outcomes?'

There is this massive, massive, massive push for targeted work and there's this massive thing, like for CAFs: 'You haven't done any CAFs, each person needs to do 'X' number of CAFs.' So there was this massive push for that. All the youth centres in the service all have to do all tick boxes and everything else, there's no choice.

It's now got to the stage where if we don't do it, you go to supervision, PDRs, and they look at you, 'How many contacts have you made?' And obviously your manager can go and see it. If you didn't meet your targets, you go into 'capability', it becomes an issue for your job. Because you may be doing good youth work in your area but if you're not showing that you're meeting your targets, you're not doing your work. That's how they perceive it.

Some workers felt powerless in the face of what feels like inevitable change.

At some point, we don't have a choice because the choice has already been taken out of our hands. All of us around the room are already using systems, whether we like it or not, to record young people's data.

It's the first time I'd really thought about it and I think it's that way for a lot of youth workers. It's just part of what we do and so we just do it. And I guess I feel we're going to be swimming against the tide because it's the direction we're going in.

There was also a feeling of isolation for those who spoke out.

I have fought in my authority, I have fought and I fight against the people to say. 'I don't agree with this, I don't think we should be doing this'... There's other people who do agree with me but they won't put their head above the parapet because they are too scared.

*They also tried to talk to me as if I was stupid which really made me cross. Because when I said, 'I take the names and addresses but why do **you** need names and addresses?' They said, 'Any project takes names and addresses.' I said, 'But **you're** not taking them, why do you need the names and addresses?'*

Compliance was seen as being linked to funding in both statutory and voluntary sectors.

If you don't play the game you won't get the money and they'll just find an excuse to cut and get rid of you. It's a really sad state of affairs to be in.

OPPOSITION

Despite the pressure described above, it would be wrong to characterise detached youth workers as passively accepting their own involvement in tracking young people. Many part-time workers and managers are actively challenging the new information sharing systems, searching for space to demonstrate their opposition.

1. Not Adding Young People's Personal Details to Shared Databases:

I don't actually fill in the forms. I don't get into trouble. My admin worker tells me that I'm rubbish, that's her line.

You don't necessarily need to get all the data they require as long as you get some evidence from the young people and produce that on your evaluation side, we play that game, we find that a stronger card to pull.

They're trying to bring ethnicity in to our end-of-session reports as well but luckily we're quite a big team so we've all said we don't feel comfortable making an assumption about young people's ethnicity, so why should we?

You can put 'Anonymous' or you can put 'Mickey Mouse' or whatever the young person's told you that their name is.

However, there was a feeling that the potential to refuse to identify young people is diminishing.

We just put everyone in as anonymous, and they've just got onto us and said, 'Who are all these anonymous people?' And we're like, 'I don't know!' And they're like, 'They can't all be anonymous', and we're like, 'They are'. So they're kind of a bit not happy with the way we've been anonymising contacts, so we're sort of in an early fight stage.

We used to put in a lot of the young people had nicknames and that was acceptable.

I've already had the argument with my Principal Officer about anonymity and young people that want to remain anonymous and obviously for my detached workers and my mobile workers I don't want them having to go out and be pressurised into getting names, addresses, postcodes. So we are still arguing with regard being able to enter people anonymously.

Its a nightmare because you can't put in anonymous group contacts or anonymous individual contacts at all, which we used to be able to do but they decided to change it and go with the newer system... We would put in their first name and then the area that they live in but now we're getting told we can't do that any more because we've got such a long list with everybody with the same surname ... so now the firmer line has been brought it that you must get dates of birth, you must get surnames, you must get addresses.

2. Refusing to Give Young People's Personal Details to Other Agencies:

Participants had increasingly found that funders and partner agencies were asking for personal details of young people, often after the funded activity had already taken place. Some workers had refused to do this or negotiated that they would share basic details only.

Just last week [another agency] offered a whole week's worth of activities and at the end of it wanted my consent forms. I was like, 'You're not having my consent forms'. He goes, 'Well, I need information off it', and I was like... 'Ask the young people if they'll give that information but I'm not giving you these'. And they wanted a whole list of postcodes, ages, sexuality, everything, and I was thinking. Why does [that agency] need that information?' So we kind of hit loggerheads there that I wasn't willing to give it.

We're working with the police and they give us all this money through the Home Office and half way through they were like, 'We need to know who's on it so we can track and monitor them'... So I told them we didn't want their money. And they were like, 'Oh, go on then, have it anyway'. And then we hit targets for the lowest crime in the area ever.

[We received] some funding so I could take some young people away and it was that whole thing at the end of it, are they at risk of this or that? I didn't just tick the boxes, I just refused, I was like, 'How comes it's any of their business?'

The forms arrived a week before the project was due to start and they wanted names, addresses, phone numbers. Attached to the bottom were tick boxes of what you believed of the young person, whether you believed them to take drugs, truant, anti-social behaviour, whether you believed that their family offended and I was just horrified at this form and my first instinct was, 'I don't want their money if I've got to do this because I'm not going to do it'. And I spoke to my line manager who was really good and he said he agreed with me... If a young person came to me and said, 'Look at this form, do you think I should fill this out?' I would be saying, 'Actually, I don't think you should put this information to your name and address'. And I know, if I had said to the young people, 'Fill the form out', they would have done because they trust me, but I didn't want to do that... What I did in the end was come up with the solution, I cut the form in half, so they had their names and addresses, but all the other information, for their statistics they had it but it wasn't connected to any young people.

3. *Educating Ourselves, Young People, Colleagues And Managers.*

One of the things which you can do locally is if you are linked up to the council maybe get the legal department to come and have a discussion with you about the Data Protection Act... Also [groups like Liberty] can run workshops with young people, ... it's all very well us starting to get a bit of enlightenment, but its also about young people maybe kicking off a little bit as well.

At the end of the day my responsibility is to my manager but I'm in youth work, so my principles are about educating people higher up than me how to work with youth. Don't just pull them in and have them as a puppet, thank you very much.

The presentation yesterday has made us more aware... and we're going to go and feed back, and they'll feed back to other people. We're going to go back and cause a riot [laughter] and I think that is really good if other people are now going to be passionate about this. I am now.

RELEVANT ORGANISATIONS

Federation for Detached Youth Work:
http://detached.youthworkonline.org.uk
Action for Rights for Children (ARCH):
http://www.arch-ed.org/
Liberty:
http://www.liberty-human-rights.org.uk/
No. 2 ID:
http://www.no2id.net/
Critically Chatting Collective:
http://criticallychatting.wordpress.com/

DATABASES:

QES:
http://www.qualityeducationsolutions.co.uk/qes_youth_services.html
Youthbase:
http://www.generic-software.com/youthbase/
Common Assessment Framework:
http://www.everychildmatters.gov.uk/deliveringservices/caf/
Contact Point:
http://www.everychildmatters.gov.uk/deliveringservices/contactpoint/

Chaos in the world brings uneasiness, but it also allows the opportunity for creativity and growth.
   –Tom Barrett

HERE'S LOOKING AT YOU KID (OR THE HOODIES FIGHT BACK)

Difficulties are meant to rouse, not discourage. The human spirit is to grow strong by conflict

–William Ellery Channing

At the time of writing, liverpool has approximately 242 CCTV cameras. Unlike Katie Melua's claim that 'there are nine million bicycles in Beijing', that is a fact. This represents the biggest CCTV system in Europe and is part of the infrastructure that fits in with a policy to extend 'surveillance and partnership interventions in target hot spots, including the introduction of 'City Watch' street crime wardens' – the strategy for 'partnership' approaches to 'regeneration'.

These expressions are interesting in themselves. 'Regeneration' suggests that there has been 'degeneration' (a 'rotting' and/or 'festering' of a former state). 'Partnership' implies, of course, that the forces that have tasked themselves to 'regenerate' will recruit those within the 'regeneration zone' to their cause. This is a kind of bureaucratic fantasy that there is a broad consensus about and understanding of what is meant by 'regeneration' across social groupings and that the belief can be promulgated among those to be controlled that any partnership between the State and those it exists to control is going to be anything but one-sided. However, increased surveillance via CCTV, tagging and ASBOs cannot prevent the response of individuals and groups to what they experience as oppressive social conditions. How can technical or procedural devices prevent the consequences of inequality, poverty and ignorance and oblige people to revise exhibited behavioural patterns? Observation and the threat that it might pose to those being observed are, by their character, only able to incite equal and opposite reactions such as concealment and defence.

For example, a few Monday evenings ago I was in Birmingham city centre and was struck by what seemed like an inordinate number of people begging. Many more than I had come across in any British context for some time. I asked a young woman (one of a number of people selling 'Big Issue' in the area) about this situation and she told me that what I was

B. Belton, Developing Critical Youth Work Theory: Building Professional Judgment in the Community Context, 131–143.

observing was a Monday and Sunday evening phenomenon that was a consequence of Community Wardens not working at those times. This reminded me of the efforts American forces made in the 1960s to prevent the Vietcong from entering South Vietnam. The US military machine destroyed the bridges crossing the many rivers that roughly divide North from South Vietnam. They sought to maintain the severed links via blanket ground, sea and aerial observation as well as intensive satellite surveillance. However, the Vietcong continued to turn up in vast numbers deep into South Vietnamese territory. It was thought that tunnels might have been the means of entry but this could not adequately explain the sheer weight of North Vietnamese forces that were appearing in the South, sometimes deploying hefty equipment. It was only after the war that the American's discovered that the North Vietnamese had built bridges across numerous rivers but they were 'invisible' bridges, built six inches under water.

Inserting a technical rationality to enforce order in place of organic, interactive, human or humane responses aimed at promoting responsibility have not and will not work in terms of instilling conformity to particular values or a commitment to establishment rules and regulations. This was part of the observation of Orwell's 'Nineteen Eighty Four' (1949). What such mechanisms promote is what might be understood as the natural or logical response to surveillance – avoidance, secrecy, concealment and stealth. Instead of advancing conformity, these devices stimulate the self-protective responses of cunning, slyness, ducking and diving. Hoodies and baseball caps are the tip of the iceberg in terms of the 'camouflaged society' that mass surveillance kindles. That these 'fashions' have been adopted as youth 'battle dress' tells a story of how young people see themselves and society- a place where everyone has something to hide even if they are not sure what it is they are concealing or from whom they are hiding.

Of course, it becomes only a matter of time before individual attempts to obscure the means of identification become offences in themselves. I was with a group of youth work students in a city centre bar in the spring of 2009 and two black women in our number were refused service because they were wearing hats. They were not clearly identifiable by the brewery's covert surveillance operation and were, in fact, punished for this by 'commercial ostracism'. Anonymity is 'offensive'. This incident also makes one aware that there are many, many more than 242 CCTV cameras in Liverpool. The level of 'privatised' surveillance of groups, individuals and communities is probably unknown but most of it can be accessed by enforcement and control bodies.

As the hoodies proliferate and are supplemented with shadow casting baseball caps, as the likes of Jack Straw struggle to find a way round the veil, hijab, niqab and burqua, mass technical observation and tracking is masked as a means of producing a more 'harmonic', peaceful or 'safe' society. The actuality is that what it creates is a social milieu premised on covert action and paranoia. The hoodies have noted this and acted as have young Muslim women in a different way. On one side, people are convinced by media and state propaganda that they are under siege from crime which can even be interpreted through 'fashion' or 'belief', while on the other side, groups (mainly of young people) develop a determination to minimise the extent they can be spied upon by often invisible observers.

Young people are becoming evermore conscious of being under 'the gaze' of ubiquitous but largely anonymous authority, provoking a reaction of a whole repertoire of 'covering up'. In this situation we, as youth workers, eulogise considerations like 'trust', 'honesty' and 'transparency', all of which might appear as part of the 'mood of the age'. Such aspects of our agenda may be seen to have the potential to increase the quality and quantity of surveillance by both young people and the 'watchers' (see the previous two chapters).

It was also in Birmingham that I spoke to a young Traveller about 'trusting' youth workers. She told me,

Oh yea, they talk about 'establishing trust' and 'building relation-ships', but they get paid don't they, by the council or whatever. Why would you trust them? They take us out and stuff but we aint got nuffin to thank them for; that's their job! They take you out and expect you to trust them because they have been nice to you and stuff, but we only tell them what they want to hear. I wouldn't tell em nuffin that was important. You can't trust any of them coz they write all that stuff about you down and you know they do that because others know what you have said to them. They know about you from them. They say 'we are honest with you' but if they were honest they won't write stuff about us that we can't see. I asked to see them notes and they won't show em to you. They say they are 'confidential'. That's shit. They just lie like everyone else. But that's ok coz we know they lying. But I don't tell them that. Best to go on letting them think we's idiots.

This might not represent a 'new consciousness' on the part of young people but it seems the more you obviously observe a group, the more suspicious that group will become of those they understand to be observing them. As surveillance grows almost unabated, the possible effects are hard to predict. Indeed, quite what kind of a society we are building, the social consequences of this incursion over a prolonged period of time, is hardly determinable. However, I'm pretty confident that there is and will be an effect and perhaps this is already happening. It's just that we can't quite see it. What seems clear is that all this needs 'looking into'.

Informal education is a complimentary facet of surveillance culture in that 'informal' in practice means 'covert'. When the informal educator approaches their client it is rare that their intention to educate is openly shared with the target. The strategies of informal education are designed not to make it look/feel like education in order that contact with the client can be maintained; the assumption being that the target (the person seen as in need of education; ignorant) as soon as they understood themselves to be an candidate for 'education' would (quite reasonably perhaps) seek to avoid the educator.

The initial phase of 'contact' is the 'intervention' the aim of which is to cultivate what is called the 'relationship' that is to be 'used' to achieve the informal educator's agenda, which is based on organisational aims and ultimately State policy/legislation.

This cannot of course be an educational procedure. Education to be education is entered into with all who are involved conscious of the 'fact' that they are involved in an educational project. In a situation wherein one person is unaware that they are being 'educated' this is an act of covert indoctrination; informal = covert, education = indoctrination. The means to do this, 'fun'/'positive' activities, entertaining diversions are forms of propaganda in that they are used for largely unstated aims. The contemporary drive in youth work towards forms of assessment and accreditation are in comparison relatively overt forms of operation compared to informal education.

The predatory nature of the informal educator's approach, the invasive character of the intervention tactic (an invasive act of interference) using the 'pretend relationship' for ulterior motives, together with the largely uninformed hypotheses about the person-made-client's relative ignorance and subsequently their psychological/emotional state, can cause the process to be interpreted as potentially an act of psychological violence (in that it has the potential to violate).

However, this is not how most youth workers operate.

ABUNDANT PRESENCE

Gopal is a centre-based youth worker in Manchester. He has been employed in the same project for around eight years. He generally comes into work around 11am and for a few hours ambles though the administrative tasks that are part of his role in a fairly relaxed but efficient way. From about mid-day young people drift into the project, many during their school lunch break. They might play pool, set up the table tennis tables for a knock about or just have a snack, a drink and watch a DVD. Sometimes they will go into Gopal's office and chat and joke with him. He often gets invited to get involved with what the young people are doing, mostly he does, but sometimes he doesn't depending on the other demands on his time.

Gopal and his part-time workers have a pretty full evening programme, but it is not unusual for this to be altered at the demand or request of young people. Mostly they prefer to use the project as a 'chill-out zone', basically a place to come and chat and pass time, have a little fun. Gopal generally goes along with this. He told me,

> *I don't see myself as an 'intervener'. In the main people know where I am and they come and seek me out when they want to. I think it is my professional duty to be there for them when they want me to be. I'd like to say I try to be 'totally responsive' but of course no one is 'totally responsive'. But for the most part I think the people who use this place know that I'm there for them. For me that is the main skill. Ha ha...they intervene with me!*

Carol and Demi are 15. They regular users of the project. They shared the following conversation with me,

Carol: *Gopal's ok. He's not 'in-your-face' like.*
Demi: *He can be a bit of a wanker though*
Carol: *But in a funny way. In a nice way*
Demi: *Oh yea – not a 'bad' wanker...ha ha*
Carol: *We take the piss out of him a bit.*
Demi: *'What you getting paid for?' we say ha ha.*
Carol: *But you can go and chat to him almost any time.*
Demi: Yea. *He always has time for people.*
Carol: *If you ask him to do anything he'll try and get it done or if you ask him about stuff he will always give you an honest answer.*
Demi: *Yea...he can make you think can't he.*
Carol: *He does my bleedin head in sometimes ha ha*
Demi: *Like he wanted us to organise this trip to France yea and he ended up doing it all and pretending to the Council that we did it all. Clever that eh?*
Carol: *Well, we did do some of it. I had to phone the ferry people and everything*
Demi: *That's coz you're a MUG girl!*
Carol: *You did the menus and everything*

Demi: *Yea, but the menus were good weren't they – you liked em. You didn't leave much on your plate!*

Carol: *That's coz Gopal sorted out Waitrose*

Demi: Na! *Derek sorted out Waitrose...He went down there from school and saw Cherry's brother, the assistant manager bloke.*

Carol: *That was Cherry's idea. And that was her uncle*

Demi: *Well Derek sorted it*

Carol: *Yea. He did all right...for a change...ha ha*

Demi: *But Gopal done most of it*

Carol: *What did he do?*

Demi: *Don't really remember...whatever*

Carol: *I think people here like that about him.*

Demi: *What? That they don't remember what he does ha ha?*

Carol: *H ha...no, that he's honest like*

Demi: *He don't bullshit you.*

Carol: *If he don't like something he will say 'I don't like that!'*

Demi: *But then if he thinks something is cool he'll tell you that too.*

Carol: *He sometimes says 'do you want to do this' and everybody says 'Nooo!' ha ha.* Demi: *But then some people will fancy it or just give it a go any way coz others have.* Carol: *But he don't force nothing on you.*

Demi: *You just think 'Gopals' there' and he is.*

Carol: *Just between us I think that's what he get's paid for ha ha...but don't tell him that ha ha.*

Demi: *He can make you think though*

Carol: *He says he 'educates' us ha ha*

Demi: *Ha ha – when he's mucking around he does*

Carol: *I reckon we bloody well educate him!*

Demi: *He says that though*

Carol: *What?*

Demi: *That we educate him*

Carol: *Well we do!*

Demi: *Yea*

Carol: *But he makes you think*

Demi: *Yea. His thinking makes you think. But he can be a wanker too*

Carol: *Derek's a wanker*

Demi: *But he's a real wanker...Gopal's not a wanker most of the time and when he is he's no a wanker like Derek...he does make you think...my head hurts sometimes ha ha*

Carol: *Who? Derek?*

Demi: *Ha ha no...Gopal...Derek's a wanker. Gopal goes something like 'So if that's like that, why you think it's like this?*
Carol: *But Derek sorted Waitrose out*
Demi: *Yea. He did that*
Carol: *But I like Derek*
Demi: *Yea I like him ok. Gopal likes Derek. He says he's 'entrepreneurial'.*
Carol: *Yea. Gopal's all right.*
Demi: *Yea.*

I questioned Gopal about being an educator:

Am I and educator? Well, I suppose that is for other people to say. My priority is that the people that use this place do so safely and that they have some fun and maybe an interesting time. I'd like to think they are 'better people' for coming here but that sounds a bit pompous. For most of them this place is just a little part of their lives for a little while.

I've heard it said by colleagues that you don't have to like the people you are working with to do a good job. That might be true, but I tell you what, it don't half help if they do like you. I like the people I work with and if they like me they will teach me about them and I think that is what gives a chance for things to work. They let me do the work because I have found out about them and they have found out things about me. Ha ha – I think we think that we know each other – but that helps a lot. But none of them are really bad kids, but what's a bad kid? People tend to be how people treat them. All of us are products of something.

Yes, maybe some people that use this place get some education from being here but they get that more from themselves and each other than from me I think. The other workers and me set up situations where this might happen I suppose. But you can't do a thing until the people that come here let you do it. They are the ones that make everything possible. So why wouldn't I like them?

No one comes here to be educated mate and they just laugh at me when I say I'm educating them. They are probably right in doing that. They come here to chill, kick-back, have a laugh, get out the house sometimes flirt a bit. That's ok isn't it? If while there are doing that they learn a bit about the world that's fine, but they would get that without this place. In places where there are no youth centres and no youth workers people still learn about life. You can't say that because of youth workers people know more about life than they did 500 years ago or than say in a village in Africa. How could you prove that?

But yea, people get something out of this place otherwise they wouldn't come back here would they? They do things together sometimes come up with new ideas, different ways of seeing what goes on. It's all good. If anything does happen it is because people do things together. You can wander into a place and say 'Hey, I'm going to educate these people' but that just won't work. Education is not something that happens to people, it is something that happens between people. Ha ha – that's what I've learnt...

This type of mutuality is the stuff of youth work. It is a means of bringing a sometimes relaxed and calm, sometimes exciting and dynamic series of humane interactions into being wherein people can be what they want to be. And what they want to be is usually a good enough basis for them to talk about their dreams, which is often the way to build their ambitions. Nothing in this is forced, nothing (to quote Carol) is 'in-your-face'. It is a kind of thoughtful dance and Gopal acts more by invitation than intervention. His professionality lies in this 'abundant presence' he provides. What Carol notes is his skill in not intervening , and his alertness to react positively to invitation, while cordially offering invitations of his own that can be taken up, declined or modified.

This stance seems a more honest, democratic, effective, mutual, natural and kind than the mechanics of informal education.

NOT SO MUCH EDUCATORS AND LEARNERS

Hala Said is a Somali Muslim youth worker in London. Part of her professional perspective is based not the direct effort to educate others but a readiness educated by others. For her this sets up an educational encounter wherein all can become more informed and even enlightened.

In Britain education is broadly connected to obtaining qualifications which largely determinate one's status in society. This academic basis means that much effort is spent collecting knowledge often without understanding its value. Anyone who does not have the ability to put their thoughts on paper in a prescribed way is in danger of being labelled a failure, while policy obliges everyone to gain at least a level 2 qualification. But this begs the question why is it that the government has the expectation that people will take part in 'lifelong learning' through community education, for example, promoting sexual health, International Women's Day and Black History Month. Who needs community education and why?

It seems that it is the State that expresses the need for community education and it appears that it is a tool to promote society's expectation of how to become 'moral' and/or a 'model' subject. Informal and community educators are rarely invited into communities by ordinary people and as such they impose education upon people, just by their presence. Cursory observation of what goes on in community education will reveal that it is used to forward State policies. Other ambitions for its use are to 'address terrorism' and what some interpret as 'extremism', while encouraging ideas of 'integration' and 'diversity'. It is also deployed to promote particular understandings of 'Britishness', the citizenship test might be understood as an example of this. This type of community education often seems to result in some immigrants having more knowledge of Britain than some British born people!

For all this, how can community educators provide education if community is made up of people from different races, cultural groups and faiths, etc? Even if a targeted community shares a culture or faith, it can be argued that each member of that particular community may not share the same values or norms. If (for instance) we look at the Somali community, this is made of numerous and different tribes and clans. Different norms and behaviors are expected in each of these groupings. However the Somali community share the experience of exclusion and labeling in the British context although segregation and division between tribes and clans continues.

This is why those looking to educate communities should be themselves ready to be educated by those communities; this could be seen as the most effective and realistic form of community education.

In the Somali community female genital-cutting (FGC – also known as 'female circumcision' or 'female genital mutilation/cutting' – FGM/C) has become an issue. The term is almost exclusively used to describe a tradition and/or a cultural/religious procedure that parents must consent to before it can be undertaken. The terminology used to refer to these procedures has changed, and the clearly disapproving and powerfully evocative expression of 'female genital mutilation' has now all but been replaced by the possibly inaccurate, but relatively less value-laden term of 'female circumcision'. However, changing the term to describe FGM is meaningless, because this did not change the concept or the practice. Unless hidden agendas are challenged, the situation will not change. Many Somalis have been obliged abandon FGM because of the law in Britain. People are loathe to challenge this law, as war is still raging in Somalia and people are anxious about maintaining their status in terms of being allowed to remain in Britain. Effectively, they fear the protection of the British State might be withdrawn from them if they break the law.

Many Somalis women are pressurized into accepting FGM as it's related to honor, status and family values. In the Somali community men hold a great deal of control over matters of honour. Islam does not sanction FGM, but most women before the early 1980s did not have access to education and were not told that FGM is not part of Islam.

The traditional cultural practice of FGC predates both Islam and Christianity. A Greek papyrus from 163 B.C. tells of how young women in Egypt underwent circumcision and the practice is widely accepted as having originated in the Nile valley at the time of the Pharaohs. Evidence from mummies has shown that FGC was practiced in antiquity; the earliest evidence of male circumcision is also from Ancient Egypt.

While little is know about how the practice of FGC spread, the procedure is now practiced by some Muslims (although it might be thought of as contrary to their religious beliefs). This said, I have found that there is a misconception among many community educators that FGM started in East Africa. However, there is a history of misinformation about the procedure. People advocating or performing these practices have claimed that young women of all ages would otherwise engage in excessive masturbation and will be 'polluted' by this activity (referred to as 'self-abuse').

In Somali culture elders have claimed that young women could be involved in sexual activities which could define them as 'loose' and/or lacking control over their sexual urges unless FGM was performed. Although masturbation is forbidden in Islam it has no clear connection to FGM.

The term 'polluted' effectively takes away the right of sexual pleasure from women. However, this is enacted by male authority; the male ego controls women by the insisting that they maintain their virginity before marriage, although according to Islam parents are ordered to look out for their daughters' honour; Allah all mighty certainly did not deem men to be in control to such an extent as he gave women authority over themselves.

FGC advocates have also argued that the practices cure females of a range of psychological diseases including depression, hysteria, insanity and kleptomania. FGC is sometimes seen as a means of control over female virtue or used as a means of preservation and proof of virginity. It is regarded in many societies and cultures as a prerequisite for honorable marriage. A husband will sometimes cut his bride's scar tissue open after marriage to allow for sexual intercourse.

Men who fail to marry circumcised women risk stigmatisation. At the same time women who have had genital surgery are often considered to have higher status than those who have not and are entitled to positions of religious, political and cultural influence and authority.

In the early 1990s, when a large numbers of Somalis migrated to Britain because of the civil war, they felt their culture was exposed. A part of the culture that was kept hidden once upon a time is now challenged. Schools, communities, doctors and so fourth discussed the impact of FGM and viewed it as child abuse. This had a negative impact on Somalis. Parents stood labeled as 'child abusers' and thus the issue became a focus of conflict between children and their parents. Many in the community have claimed that forms of British community education brought this type of stigma, resulting in depression and other psychological issues.

It might be argued that community educators confronted the situation for the 'greater good', however the approach of community education together with the trauma of migration and the accompanying social challenges were a great burden to Somalis.

FGC has been a specific criminal offence in United Kingdom since the Prohibition of Female Circumcision Act was passed in 1985. This was superseded by the Female Genital Mutilation Act 2003. The Scottish Parliament also passed the Prohibition of Female Genital Mutilation (Scotland) Act in 2005, but the procedure remains an enduring tradition in many societies and cultural groups in the UK. Political leaders have found it difficult to eliminate at local levels because of its cultural and sometimes political significance. Because FGC has strong cultural and marital consequences, its opponents recognize that in order to end the practice it is necessary to work closely with local communities.

Informal educators are largely unaware and uneducated about FGM. For example, in my practice area a worker expressed her concern for young Somali female whose family took her back to Africa for a year. The worker contacted social services for advice and wrote a letter to the youth service department highlighting this situation as a child protection matter.

I took a stand to challenge this person, although it can be said that she was merely following British law and what was expected of her as a youth worker. Nonetheless, she had no clear understanding of FGM. I called a team meeting hoping that as colleagues we might educate each other. Some staff had never heard of FGM while others believed it to be strongly linked with the Somali community and Islamic culture. There was no under-standing of the cultural background that might allow an approach to this community in an empathic way (which is a basic youth work skill). The staff members described FGM as 'child abuse' and taking away women's rights. They claimed that Islam is not promoting women's rights.

I listened throughout the meeting and tried to explain that FGM started in Egypt and that it has no necessary link with Islam. I also made it clear that women have rights in Islam but as in some other faiths women's rights were being demolished by the fact that men create the law not faith. I made the point that young Somali women need to be approached with sensitivity and empathy not just to promote law and policy awareness, but with an understanding of the psychological factors involved in FGM, keeping the well-being/welfare of young people in mind, particularly when the term 'child abuse' is aimed at parents who consent to the practice. Finally I talked about being aware of equal opportunity and child protection law.

My team left the meeting with a clearer understanding after a long debate. This exemplified that informal educators and other practitioners need to be educated by members of the communities they work with long before they seek to themselves educate those same communities.

The next day there were comments on my desk asking me to carry out community education in the Somali community focusing on FGM as it was seen that I was 'perfect to promote awareness'. My reply to that was the community needs to settle in Britain before an awareness of law and legislation in Britain can be imposed upon them. Again, there was an agenda to 'educate' people (which assumed ignorance) without really understanding or being ready to be educated by them.

Most people in the Somali community became aware in early 1990s that FGM is not sanctioned in Islam and causes major health complications, particularly when giving birth. This undermines the conclusion that Somalis are uneducated/uninformed about FGM. Why is this in question? Why are Somalis seen to lack this awareness? Because some parts of the community still practice FGM knowing the Islamic view, the health issues and the law? It is still linked with the cultural concept of purity and virginity!

It is unrealistic to expect Somalis to accept the law and demolish all the cultural beliefs so swiftly. As Malcolm X argued, we seem to use scientific theory to deal with the self or consciousness. In his last speech he said,

> *I think all of us should be critics of each other. Whenever you can't stand criticism you can never grow. I don't think that it serves any purpose for the leaders of our people to waste their time fighting each other needlessly. I think that we accomplish more when we sit down in private and iron out whatever differences that may exist and try and then do something constructive for the benefit of out people. But on the other hand, I don't think that we should be above criticism. I don't think that anyone should be above criticism.*

It is very important to learn from each other; from young people and the community itself to benefit people and ourselves. Unless education occurs as a two way process then it is not effective education – it is just another form of psychological manipulation.

The above demonstrates and is representative of something of the everyday perspectives and practice of youth workers. This is not set in the mechanics of community and informal education but in the realistic flow of life and mutual interaction. Like Hala and Gopal, youth workers tend to find the most effective ways to work with the people they come into contact with; there is a discernable impact of professional culture that is an intellectual resource in their practice.

Looking at actual examples of youth work thinking and activity can reveal the humane and dynamic character of the work, showing it to be a much more of a cooperative, collaborative endeavour than it is an interventive operation. But maybe we are professional Hoodies or have something in common with the fear around status loss that Hala refers to. Much youth work activity largely remains hidden because it might not be understood as following organizational or State agenda and as such we might feel obliged to either disguise practice or just follow prescriptions like those embedded in the proposal of informal and community education. This is understandable, but it risks youth work becoming extinct as definite and distinct, interrelative, humanitarian pursuit.

Freedom of the mind requires not only, or not even especially, the absence of legal constraints but the presence of alternative thoughts. The most successful tyranny is not the one that uses force to assure uniformity, but the one that removes awareness of other possibilities
– Alan Bloom

BIBLIOGRAPHY

Gibb, J. (2005). *Who's watching you?: The chilling truth about the state, surveillance and personal freedom.* Collins & Brown.

Hernlund, Y., & Shell-Duncan, B. (Eds.). (2007). *Transcultural bodies: Female genital cutting in global context.* Rutgers University Press.

Lyon, D. (2006). *Theorizing surveillance: The panopticon and beyond.* Willan Publishing.

Lyon, D. (2007). *Surveillance studies: An overview.* Polity Press.

Orwell, G. (2004). *Nineteen eighty-four.* Penguin Classics; New Ed.

Rahman, A., & Toubia, M. (2000). *Female genital mutilation: A guide to laws and policies worldwide.* Zed Books Ltd.

X, M. (1989). *Malcolm X: The last speeches.* Pathfinder.

CHE GUEVARA AND THE MODIFICATION
OF OLD DOGMAS

*The liberals in the House strongly resemble liberals I have known
through the last two decades in the civil rights conflict. When it comes
time to show on which side they will be counted, they excuse
themselves.*

—Shirley Chisholm

In an article called *What is a Guerrilla Fighter?* written in 1959, Ernesto
Guevara was to call the armed victory of the Cuban people during that
country's civil war that concluded that year 'a modifier of old dogmas.' In
this chapter I will be looking at the relevance of Guevara's ideas and
philosophy to youth work that, at its most effective, has a tradition of
'working between the cracks'. I will refer to 'fighting' and the 'enemy'
because these words were part of Che's guerrilla lexicon. However, in
terms of this chapter these words are metaphoric and symbolic of the
obstacles and challenges, organizational, structural, political, policy related
and human that the youth worker might come across during the course of
their career. I will attempt to take on the spirit of Guevara's endeavour
of half a century ago and apply it to youth work in the contemporary
community context.

I have long believed youth work to be something of a 'guerrilla'
profession in practice (if not in 'official' intention). Indeed, the current
threats to its very existence might be understood as a consequence of youth
work's propensity to break away from the purposes that the profession has
traditionally been intended and funded to serve.

The continuing problem with youth workers as 'cuddle police' is that
they persistently 'go native' which has historically been an issue with
'colonial forces' and as such a threat to 'Empire'. Empires usually attempt
to eradicate elements that potentially contradict or challenge their logic.

History has shown Che Guevara's theories, laid out in his book
Guerrilla Warfare, to be strategic studies of genius, wrought out of
practical experience. That they can be understood by almost anybody and
have proved to be adaptable to a range of environments (the latest being

B. Belton, *Developing Critical Youth Work Theory: Building Professional Judgment in the Community Context, 145–164.*

youth work) has made them devastatingly effective. These writings were and continue to be revolutionary in that they have changed the way war is waged. Indeed, the modern battle, in the contemporary world, is almost a thing of the past.

Guevara's work on guerrilla fighting provides a template for the action of a few people that can be used to grab victory from a well equipped army. His writing on the subject demonstrates that a basic knowledge of people and geography can overcome the most contemporary technological weapons. Relatively poor resources, minimal initial popular support and limited communications are, for Che, no reason not to begin a resistance movement able to occupy the efforts of a regular army at the same time as gaining new recruits to the cause.

Weapons of mass destruction are inappropriate, blunt weapons when it comes to putting down jungle, mountain or urban guerrillas. Tanks and heavy artillery are also often more of a hindrance than a help fighting in mountainous or forested areas.

'Guerrilla' means 'little war' in Spanish and that is what Che designs as a means to bringing down great monolithic forces. One's effort goes into making the war small. Just as a boxer with a limited repertoire but plenty of heart and determination will cut down the ring space against a versatile opponent, pushing them onto the ropes and into corners, keeping the fight close, Che instructed forces with restricted means but a powerful cause to pick their ground and disallow their enemy the room and the horizon they needed to be effective. I do not believe that youth workers can change society nor can they prevent considerations like teenage pregnancy and knife crime. We are patently not equipped to be able to meet such massive social tasks. But we can and do fight 'little wars'. Our role is local and limited, but this also means it can be diffuse and widespread, taking place in any number of locations right across a regional or national prospect, as well as focused at an area level. The authentic achievements of our work happen in the 'here' and 'now'. They effect how a person feels about themselves and others in the relatively small portion of their lives that we see them for. This should not be overestimated but neither should it be undervalued. In *Voyage of the Dawn Trader* by C.S. Lewis, Ramandu, a star, on being told by Eustace Clarence Scrubb that *In our world a star is a huge ball of flaming gas* replies *Even in your world, my son, that is not what a star is but only what it is made of.* Likewise, you and I are made of flesh, blood, and sinew, but that is not who we are; we are something more. So the collective impact of 'bits' youth work will not be negligible – ten thousand little things done is a big thing done.

Che's success in the context of Cuba has inspired many other revolutionary movements and his ideas have gained authority worldwide being repeatedly played out in Vietnam, Algeria, Malaya, Peru, Bolivia, Guatemala, Colombia, Venezuela, the Philippines, Northern Ireland and Nicaragua. The revival of the ANC's operations, following a string of reversals, was built around what that organisation learnt from visiting Vietnam after that nation's struggle with the USA. The Vietcong had used and adapted Guevara's methods and these were passed on to the anti-apartheid fighters. His writing has even served as a textbook for the American Green Berets as well as other North American special forces and is still being referred to by all sides of the conflicts in both Afghanistan and Iraq.

Che's theories on guerrilla warfare have captured the popular imagination and proved effective in resisting domination, often overcoming some of history's most modern and powerful forces that were seemingly equipped to obliterate any opponent. This would probably have not been possible without Che's thinking and experience.

COLONIZED YOUTH AND 'DEPENDENCY'

I believe that Che's ideas have, at least in part, albeit pretty unself-consciously, been adapted to youth work because we serve what is, essentially a colonized group and almost always without anywhere near adequate resources. Young people are, like the colonized, not seen as 'whole' (see Fanon 1967 and above) fully formed or developed. Labels like 'inexperienced', 'developing', 'childish', 'adolescent' and 'immature' confirm this with the latter three often being used as insults. However, I have known plenty of very mature 13 year olds and quite a few immature 40-somethings. I have come into contact with adults that have not had the breadth of experience that some young teenagers have. As such, these 'deficit labels' do not hold much water. It is worth bearing in mind that colonizers often referred to the 'natives' as 'children'. Some slave owners referred to their 'property' in the same manner.

For all this, the youngest baby is a fully formed being. It has all it needs to exist. Yes, she is dependent on others but we are all dependent on others. As I turn on the computer I am using to write these words I am dependent on those who dig the raw material out of the ground to generate the energy that enables the machine to 'come to life'. I am also dependent on all the intermediaries that effectively transform those raw materials into these words, including generations of intellectual, scientific and technological labour that have created computers. What makes what I'm doing possible is dependency. Dependency is a condition of modern humanity and to start measuring if a child or teenager is more dependent than me, an adult, feels like a pointless exercise. Hence, the aim often ascribed to youth workers (not unusually by youth workers themselves) 'to make young people less dependent' seems a little vain. A person is going to *make* another person less dependent? Dependency is as enriching as independence. I want those I love and care for to know they can 'depend' on me and I'd like to think that to a certain extent I can depend on them. But I and they still have areas of our lives wherein we act relatively independently. Most facets of our existence are like this. There are those who prefer always to be passive or dominant when making love but perhaps in terms of 'variety being the spice of life' taking turns is this respect might be advantageous to many. It is at least worth a try maybe?

Overall, dependency is not a 'lack' and experience is not something particular age groups have a monopoly on. At the same time, maturity is to a great extent a state of mind and reliant on as many social factors as it is on biological determinants. Slavery as an institution depended on the eugenicists' invention of race and the 'people hierarchy' that went with what Ashley Montagu (1946) called 'Man's Most Dangerous Myth' and colonization, if it was to endure, had to be premised on the 'native' being not as 'fully formed' as the colonizer. Colonial structures thus made it a God-given duty of the latter to patronize, i.e. control, the former and, in a similar fashion, the 'child' or 'youth' is identified, by his/her nature, as 'less' than the adult. Correspondingly, the civil rights and position in law of the young person is far more restricted than the adult who, in the main, is seen as responsible for having duties towards those under a certain age who are not adult.

THE DEFICIT MODEL

The 'deficit model' is central to the colonizing process. If any other group were restricted in the way young people are we would be justifiably disturbed about their lack of civil rights. Let's imagine Britain's population was 25 percent Mexican and we didn't allow the Mexicans to vote, have sex, watch certain forms of entertainment, enter pubs, buy cigarettes, drive, own property, go to work, pay tax. At the same time we force them attend a particular institution five days a week during daylight hours and have a non-Mexican be wholly responsible for them. Would we not be signing the petition in support of Mexican civil rights? This is not saying young people, like the rest of us, should not be subject to criminal and decency laws, but for the most part they are not, as adults are responsible for them.

This short imaginative exercise may demonstrate that it might be surprising if young people's day-to-day experience, although perhaps not as extreme as some colonial situations, did not provoke similar responses to those in openly colonized environments. In fact, so called 'youth crime', 'vandalism' and 'hooliganism' as well as fashion and music are significant as expressions of rebellion against and resistance to forms of adult domination and hegemony.

THE YOUTH WORKER AS GUERRILLA

Che starts *Guerrilla Warfare* (1960) with the statement that the Cuban Revolution 'proved the people's ability to free themselves from an oppressive government through guerrilla warfare.'

This is a powerful message that might resonate with youth workers in that it emphasizes the capability of individuals and collectives to lay the ground and take action to implement their own liberation. Guevara's claim is that in the face of all the odds, an oppressed or dominated group can free themselves from tyranny by their own activity.

He continues,

1. *Popular forces can win a war against an army.*
2. *It is not always necessary to have to wait for a revolutionary situation to arise; this can be created by a revolutionary focus.*
3. *In the underdeveloped countries of the Americas, rural areas are the best battlefields for armed struggle.*

These ideas are founded on an optimistic belief but also the fact of the success of the Cuban revolution. For Che, if popular forces can win a war against an army, then 'the do-nothing attitude' of those he called 'pseudo-revolutionaries' (and I guess we might all know a few of those) is inherently flawed.

Guevara argued that if a revolutionary situation can be created then there is no need to wait until all the required conditions for a theoretical Marxist revolution are ripe. This was against the credo of most official Communist parties at the time.

However, Che argued that the small guerrilla force in outlying, relatively non-industrialised areas can only operate on one absolute condition – as an armed vanguard requiring popular support beyond the short term. With this advantage in place the guerrilla force cannot be outnumbered by the national army although it may not have the fire-power of State forces. While the guerrilla group can call on the help of the majority of the people, the army can only call on the relatively small group of people who claim political control of the armed forces and police and who usually have the backing of a foreign or former colonial power. This being the case, in situations wherein the people, or at least the local population, are behind and support the revolutionary force, the guerrillas should prevail. Hence the youth worker's initial focus is 'the local' and the immediate.

For Che, the whole guerrilla campaign should be planned in three phases:
A. *Survival and adaptation to conditions of guerrilla life.*
B. *Erosion of enemy strength in the area marked out by the guerrilla group for its own territory.*
C. *Attacks on the enemy on their own ground, concentrating blows on communications and bases.*
Adapting Che's position to youth work;

1. *Popular forces can prevail over those with more fire-power.*
A. *Survival and adaptation to conditions of guerrilla life.*

The support and sympathy of people across an area acts as a fulcrum to adapt government, local authority or organizational policy to transform what are agenda designed to achieve control of the people into the means for people to gain access to benefits (in the widest sense of the word) shape services and/or direct resources to their particular wants/needs.

Policy designed to control	Transformed into	The means to gain access to benefits or shape services

For example, the Dockland Athletics Club (DAC – this name has been changed for the sake of confidentiality among other things) was managed by a committee and served by local authority paid officials. The committee directed a paid coaching staff numbering around eight, all of whom were PE teachers from local schools. The membership of the club was relatively small, made up of elite athletes from schools mostly in the better off eastern end of the borough of Dockland (although the club itself was based just inside the poorer, industrially run-down and less commercially developed south west of the borough). There was a growingly significant number of young black athletes from the north of the borough who were served by a volunteer coach but this group had little to do with the management or social side of the club.

Two young coaches (one male, one female) emerged as volunteers from the club membership. Both were from the least well off, most southerly part of the borough. They brought new members from that area into the club as well as a contingent from a neighboring borough (let's call it 'Castle Villages') where the two coaches were involved in youth work. Some of these people's parents also became members of the club, running a canteen and helping with coaching, social and athletic events.

2. *It is not always necessary to have to wait for a revolutionary situation to arise; this can be created by a revolutionary focus.*
B. *Erosion of enemy strength in the area marked out by the guerrilla group for its own territory.*

After a while this new membership, along with many of the original members, began to broaden the activity base of the club. Visits to more generic agencies servicing young people were organized as well as educational and social events. This was swiftly disapproved of by the committee who called on the Docklands Borough Youth Office to deal with the influx of 'non-borough' members. The Castle Villages Youth Office was contacted and the two coaches were reprimanded for using their contacts with the youth of that borough to take advantage of Dockland's services. However, by this point the 'old guard' at DAC were in the minority as a whole new membership from all over Dockland borough had been recruited. The ethnic, gender and social mix (and interaction) of the club had been radically changed. Many members had little athletic ability but all contributed to club events and its general life.

C. Attacks on the enemy on their own ground, concentrating blows on communications and bases.

After the committee tried to clamp down on the 'dizzying diversification of activity' the club was now involved in and following a massive local fund raising campaign in conjunction with two large local youth clubs and a football-based tour of Holland, the club's membership voted out the old committee and filled it with its own representatives, both parents and young people.

3. Relatively underdeveloped areas are the most suitable battlefields for struggle.

The first act of the new committee was to dismiss all the paid coaches and replace them with qualified volunteers and encouraged older members and parents to get involved with training in youth work and coaching. Local Councillors and MPs were then petitioned to back the committee's recommendation that the resources formally used to pay coaches be given to the club as seed funding for development of the facility for the use of all young people of the area. This was effectively achieved.

Over a four year period, the entire profile of the club had changed. Athletics had become just one of many reasons why people attended. The area around the club, particularly to the south, had relatively few community facilities, so when the club opened its doors (or had them opened) the membership had risen from around 40 to several hundreds with many more attending events and activities associated with the club. Finances had gone from dingy red to shining black. The facility on club nights had been transformed from a sparsely populated, echoing savanna into a noisy bustling community arena wherein people trained, played and socialized.

As can be seen from Che's analysis and the above example, a guerrilla fighter is more than a guerrilla. They are a social reformer taking up arms for the people with the aim of changing the order of things. To be efficient they must have detailed knowledge of the area of operation so that they can withdraw rapidly and hide with ease. At the same time, guerrillas need to be aware that the regular army's aim is to destroy each and every one of them; their first aim is to discover the army's strategy and to thwart it. As a youth worker knowing your area of practice, where facilities are and where people live is an essential part of professional awareness. But it is also useful to know the 'organisational geography' or practice policy. The following are 'themes' that were adopted by the Dockland Youth Service for its staff to adhere to;

- *Health and Wellbeing*
- *The Wider World*
- *Transitions – School and Beyond*
- *Cultural Awareness*
- *Citizenship/Political Education*
- *Anti-Discrimination/Equal Opportunities.*

The youth workers and coaches at the Dockland Athletic Club managed to 'tick all the boxes' in terms of these themes and indeed made their case to change and expand the agency's activity partly on the basis of following these 'themes'. You might find it useful to look back on DAC's activity and identify how it addressed the above themes.

The guerrilla, for Che, should avoid engaging in an action unless s/he is certain to succeed, using all the weak points of the enemy. You might be able to see how these goals were achieved by the DAC youth workers and coaches. However, in this situation the Dockland Youth Service also expected those working under its authority/funding to work with young people to:

- *make their own decisions*
- *acquire a range of skills, including social ones*
- *address issues of inequality*
- *learn about relationships*
- *explore values*
- *take responsibility for their own lives*
- *express their views.*

Again, you may be able to identify how DAC might have accomplished these aims. DAC quickly saw that, in terms of what it wanted to achieve, these aims that the 'colonizing force' had for 'the natives' were also weak points to be exploited and used against them. This again fits in with Che's advice for the guerrilla in that he saw the main supply of the guerrilla force's weapons coming from the army they are fighting against (pick up the enemy's weapons and use them against them). Thus the enemy will help to destroy itself. As the guerrilla has the enemy's guns, captured ammunition can also be used against the enemy.

STRIKE AND GET OUT

Guevara believed that the guerrilla needed to stick to a strategy of 'strike and get out.' This is interesting in terms of youth work in that it is almost impossible to effect lasting change at a local level as this is a contradiction in terms; constant change is inevitable (what might be changed will be changed again into something else). Che argued that guerrilla warfare is an early stage of classical warfare and as such cannot, by itself, win a war. So, as argued above, the primary objective of youth workers is not to change the world but to work with and for the people in an immediate way and on a local scale. The defeat of the oppressor's army is a long-term aim for Che.

The Dockland Athletic Club continued to grow and diversify and eventually merged with the large County Athletic Club who had lost its premises. The merger of the management committees (to form the County & Dockland Athletic Club) led to negotiations with the City authority to improve the club's amenities. The track was closed for over a year while a new surface was laid. Stands and general facilities were demolished to make way for improvements. During the closure a minimal programme of athletic events and training was arranged based at other clubs, mostly involving County Athletic Club personnel who had better networks in the athletics world. The two coaches who had started the 'Dockland Revolution' (as it was known) gained employment as full time youth workers in different parts of the country.

Those who were not 'good performers', in terms of athletics, quickly found themselves sidelined and many former DAC members drifted away from the club, with the consequence that parental involvement fell off dramatically. When the new Dockland Stadium opened, it housed a conventional elite athletics club. It was also used for sports days by local schools and as a jogging track for the newly built leisure club to the south of the site. Most of the membership did not come from Dockland borough, generally driving in along the busy A road from the county beyond the borough's eastern border where the County Club had formally been based.

This conclusion did not undermine what happened in Dockland, the quality of the work and what it achieved in terms of young people and community members experiencing how they could use their influence to take authority. Some of the young people involved have since become youth and social workers or coaches themselves and a number of the families that were instrumental in creating change at the club continue to be active in other local projects.

DAC was never going to survive as a piece of work in itself because it was a revolutionary phenomenon existing in a larger environment that was not sympathetic to its form (a bit like the Paris Commune: see *The Paris Commune Told in Pictures* http://www.katardat.org/marxuniv/2002-COMPARIS/comparis-text/comparis-strip.html). But the spores that were produced by the club have continued to spread, providing the means for other individuals and communities to likewise 'strike and get out', generating a progeny of resistance and development.

This stays true to Che's outlook as he saw guerrilla warfare being as much a training ground as anything else, a situation that can develop a nucleus of rebels, working as a small, efficient, disciplined group, capable of fighting regular battles against the army of the forces of exploitation. The point is not to 'win' any particular skirmish but to build a general purpose among as many people as possible to overcome domination and invent the means to firstly 'counter-exploit' and then undermine social systems that are inherently inhumane and not having the benefit and wishes of individuals, groups and communities at the centre of their rationale.

In order to achieve the kind of situation within an overall revolutionary movement that Che envisaged, each guerrilla becomes their own 'general' who carries with them the duty to defend their own life as carefully as a general does. With this in mind, the youth worker who openly boasts of their own 'subversive' activity (and these people exist is surprisingly large numbers) can be seen as a liability to themselves, their colleagues and those they work among. Open refusal to follow policy guidelines or just leaving a job because it does not meet with one's own 'moral code' is often neither professional nor an act of dissidence. In fact, it can be a basically irresponsible and selfish act which merely plays along with the logic of control. The potentially effective worker (in terms of 'picking up the enemy's weapons and using these against them') will not mark themselves out as a rebel to make themselves either a target or a means of tokenism.

Merely moving on to the next post because this position does not suit my profile, standing as I do on higher ethical ground, might be little more than the sign of self indulgence. Just walking away does not make things better. It only leaves that job to someone else or makes way for someone unprepared to do much more than deliver policy unquestioningly.

Becoming one's own 'general' might be thought of as developing one's professional judgment. That is what this chapter and this book is about. Critical and questioning engagement with the world creates an informed and proactive professional that is not confined to merely following the same old well-trodden paths but who is firstly able to navigate themselves along 'roads less travelled' and eventually develop the capacity to make novel and exciting new routes for themselves. In this way, they can hopefully outflank 'the enemy'.

Che makes a distinction between the regular soldier and the guerrilla fighter. 'Each guerrilla must be ready to die, not to defend an ideal, but to transform it into a reality.' Now no one is expecting youth workers to actually die for the cause despite the fact that many effectively passed away as effective practitioners through low morale and the exhaustion of trying to achieve tasks that have never been possible for them, such as preventing knife crime. But using this notion as a metaphor, maybe some of the best of our work is produced by bringing a bit of ourselves to our professional interactions. At the same time, finding a role that lives up to our personal morality might be a bigger ask than doing what we can to moderate and mediate organizational aims and institutional policy that are not as useful as they might be to those we work with, for and among.

For all this, youth work carried out in relatively unfavourable conditions is typical rather than exceptional. The profession has developed its traditions and profile in the context of being under-resourced. As such it has much in common with the guerrilla's situation. This being the case, it is not surprising that Che's campaign rules can set powerful rhetorical and metaphorical agenda for youth workers.

Strike the Enemy Constantly

Any piece of practice can be subjected to analysis and questioning in terms of its benefits or otherwise for those we work with and for. To simply deliver straightforward policy initiatives with a 'one size fits all', 'standardised' mentality is to be unprofessional. Professionals, as part of their employment identity and ethic, need to apply professional judgment i.e. critical opinion, mediated by knowledge and evidence.

Give them the Impression that they are being Harassed and Encircled

It is an almost infallible maxim in youth work that nothing happens without repeatedly requesting and when appropriate, demanding action. Local Councillors, MPs and MEPs as community representatives exist to be lobbied and activated in terms of practice needs. Policy practically begs to be interpreted rather than merely obeyed according to one single understanding.

Teach the Local Population the Aims of the Guerrilla Band so that the People can see their Advantage in Aiding the Insurrection

Before the widespread introduction of 'informal education' into youth work, many practitioners saw at least part of their role as 'social and political' education. This tended to mean in practice promoting a broadly questioning attitude that sometimes led to detailed examination of situations and consequences of both immediate and more global concern. At best these two ends could be joined to ignite and incite enough to motivate action. This is dialectical and as such dynamic rather than dialogical and static. Dockland Athletic Club could be seen as an incidence of this type.

Use Sabotage to Demoralize the Enemy and Paralyse them by Cutting off their Communications

'Sabotage' is a term borrowed from French syndicalists by American labour organizations at the turn of the 20th century. It means the hampering of productivity and efficiency. In terms of youth work, this might be understood as assisting individuals, groups and communities in examining and questioning decisions that effect them rather than just accepting direct implementation. This may feel 'demoralizing' for authority figures who have a vested interest in enacting their wishes without the inclusion ('interference') of those directly effected by the same. However, what is experienced as 'demoralizing' for one group is often 'morale enhancing' for others.

Informing the likes of local authorities, pressure and rights groups, media, mayoral offices, councillors, MPs and MEPs of wide constituent disapproval via alternative arguments for or against proposed commercial or State incursions into a neighbourhood, for example, negatively affects the direct and unmediated communication particular interests might otherwise have enjoyed with these guardians of the public interest and conduits of authority.

This is not activity confined to the youth worker. Outside guerrilla-held ground, civilian action includes raising funds, promoting and spreading information about the revolution, gaining sympathizers and information and carrying out sabotage. Guevara sees reporting news as a vital part of the guerrilla campaign. Newspapers and radio need to get the truth of events at all costs. The object of the guerrilla use of the media is to pass on the facts about the situation because the government media will certainly be lying. At the same time the social programme of the guerrillas has to be explained. Getting information about the enemy is another necessity.

Avoid Useless Acts of Terrorism

In practice any number of issues arise, but in most cases a choice exists about how they might be tackled. Youth workers often describe their tasks in terms of 'attacking', 'fighting', 'struggling', 'challenging' and 'confronting' and their 'foe' are 'oppression', 'exploitation', 'racism', 'sexism', 'homophobia' and 'bullying' among many others. This is 'high octane' language that can intimidate those we work with, possible non-professional allies and fellow professionals.

A school-based worker told me about how she was 'fighting for a young person's right not to be oppressed' while 'struggling to challenge and confront sexism' after a young women had told her about how a weekend school outing had left without her, even though she had turned up at the prearranged departure time. The youth worker also told how a young man had taken this young woman's place (eight young men and four young women had actually taken the trip). The 'battle' took weeks to 'fight' and many hours of the youth worker's time. Telephone calls and emails involved accusations, recriminations and arguments.

In a subsequent conversation with one of the teachers who had organized the trip, the young woman concerned had revealed that she had deliberately decided not to turn up for the trip as she had a chance to cover a Saturday job for someone who did go. She had told the youth worker that she had been 'left behind for no reason' during a conversation about 'being fed up with school'. She had hoped that this might 'get her out of trouble' for not turning up for the trip, deflecting blame on to the teachers who had organized the trip. She also disliked the young man who had taken her place.

While one might understand this young woman's actions and fears, even if the situation hadn't panned out this way, it is hard to see what the youth worker might have positively achieved that would have outweighed the alienation and defensiveness provoked by effectively naming the teachers' practice in this situation as being an 'oppressive' form of 'sexism'. In the end it seemed that the tactics used were always going to result in not much more than the potential loss of an ally rather than a civil liberties victory.

According to Che, each guerrilla is advised to show impeccable moral conduct and strict self-control. The guerrilla is sustained by a simple and direct purpose and ideal but not an elaborate or visionary one. Firm and clear, but not necessarily lofty direction is required – the more concrete the goal, the firmer the resolution of the guerrilla will be.

Do not Try to Hold too Much Territory

The Dockland Athletic Club had been able to sustain its practice up to the point when it looked to extend the same via a merger with the County Athletic Club, partly as a means to oblige a large investment in facilities and plant. This almost immediately involved a new range of interests and agendas.

After the merger the vanguard of change in DAC were suddenly part of a larger group, most of who wanted to continue with the traditions of the County club rather than adopt the style and approach of the Dockland club. The County club also had a substantial network within athletics to backup this position. At the same time the city authorities would hardly have invested in the seemingly amorphous (clearly revolutionary) aims of DAC. If a new athletics facility was to be built, there would be a need for a deal of assurance that it was going to be used for athletics on a city-wide scale rather than a voluntary youth work facility engaged in user and local control. In short, the Dockland club had bitten off more than what was essentially a 'guerrilla force' could reasonably have been expected to chew. As a rule of thumb, the more resources the State puts into an organization the more it will want to make sure its output complies with State agenda. Youth work is thus compromised as a guerrilla profession when and if it is sucked up into massive resource initiatives.

Che emphasizes the need for guerrillas to make their own territory into a 'little State' and a base of operations. This is much more the focus than ideas about 'growth', 'development' or 'expansion', three notions that few community organizations seem able to distinguish between (often to their cost). At times, resolution, reconciliation, rationalization, conciliation and even retreat might be much more 'developmental' than say simple 'growth'.

Create new guerrilla groups when sufficient recruits join. These new groups will hold more territory, until the offensive against the army on its own ground can start

The lesson of the above scenario is that there had not been time for sufficient numbers of activists to arise out of the membership of the Dockland club. There were not enough personnel to carry on and develop its culture beyond its existing boundaries. While it did produce a number of 'politicised' and motivated people, it overstretched its human resources and probably, in Che's terms, took on the army on its own ground. For all this, Guevara asserts that while the likes of the United States might be able to invade and inflict damage on Cuba, the Revolution would survive because it had kept its promises to the Cuban people who would defend the Revolution.

All this said, Che saw that in all conditions, tactics must be adapted to circumstances. From the youth worker's point of view this is about developing one's professional judgment, deciding on the appropriate action by and for particular people at the most suitable time. The guerrilla force needs to improvise constantly, transforming all incidents to its own advantage, which is one of the most long standing traditions and skill sets of youth work. We can moan about conditions forever with no solid outcomes or we can make use of what we have to make conditions better. Professional judgment means taking authority. Blindly following instructions and shrugging shoulders, muttering 'What can you do?' is as unprofessional as disobeying clear managerial directives in that it gives up one's professional authority. Fouling job descriptions has hardly ever achieved anything in the long run.

This paves the way for another of Che's precepts of guerrilla warfare, that classical war has to be left to the enemy. Guerrillas need to be unpredictable, all assaults are characterized by their speed. The essential elements of the guerrilla group are the use and understanding of the following...

Surprise

One of the now mostly forgotten phrases that guided youth work some years ago was 'make the familiar strange and the strange familiar'. The ability to surprise and be surprised keeps our work relevant. Being surprised by those we work with, for and among goes some way to helping us not to take people for granted. Everyone is unique, coming to us with their own history, desires, wants and needs and, somewhere, the wish to distinguish between a want and a need. This is the glorious strangeness of people that is perhaps familiar to us all.

Deception

Looking at the work and thoughts of Nicholas Estephane and Tania de St Croix (above) it is clear that dealing with and understanding deception is part of our work. But as the 'school trip' situation (detailed above) indicates, it is something human beings do to protect themselves and others that it is often understandable given former experiences or misunderstandings. However, part of our safeguarding brief and child protection procedures is that while including risk taking and excitement in our programmes, we have to ensure the safety of those we work with and for. This is something of a contradiction in terms and action. Safety is, although some of us want it some of the time, ultimately boring. To live a life worth living involves taking risks. But while there is legislation and oceans of policy relating to safety, there is often little in terms of the definite requirements of job descriptions and organizational aims that demand that we implicate risk in our practice. Yet lasting and well subscribed youth work nearly always builds in experiences that are fun, exciting and, therefore, often risky.

At the same time much of youth work needs to be justified in terms of form-filling linked to funding (see above). For instance, some time ago I heard a youth worker justifying the provision of a pool table in his agency. He told how it 'enhanced team work' and 'cooperation' (organization skills) among young people. It also acted as a 'decision making tool' (who would play and when). It had positive effects in terms of developing arithmetic (keeping and calculating scores) and geometric abilities (angles and position), while heightening 'awareness of basic physics' (trajectory, force, impact and how the relationship between speed and direction produce velocity). There were also 'therapeutic benefits' in facilitating relaxation and concentration. However, none of this was identified by the young people concerned who wanted a pool table because 'the liked playing pool'.

While some might see this as ethically questionable (and it is), for Che among the guerrilla's primary considerations is the civilian population and local custom. This 'care' allows the guerrillas to prove their *moral* superiority over the enemy. This said, there is nearly always more than one way to explain a situation. To a scientist, well versed in laws of thermodynamics, a kettle boils because the heat from the element inside the kettle has heated the water causing molecular change. But to me the kettle is boiling because I fancy a cup of tea.

For all this, Che emphases the need for civilians to understand the ideas behind the revolutionary movement. One of youth work's biggest contributions as a medium for social and political education has been the means it has provided for young people to work out just what it is that they are being deceived about.

Night Operations

A great deal of youth work happens after dark. Daytime for most young people is taken up by school, college and/or work. But more than this practical consideration, young people have historically taken youth work services in their 'own time' (although this has changed somewhat over the last decade). That is, they have seen youth work as having something they want or can use. When this becomes wholly not the case, youth work will have ceased to be youth work and will have transformed into just another form of compulsory, albeit covert, education.

AMBUSH

Che also wrote about how ambushes were part of guerrilla tactics. An ambush is a sort of animation of deception and it is often as well for youth workers as community activists not to reveal their strategies to those who might not be acting in the best interests of the community until a right time and place has been identified.

A worker was working with a community group who were involved in contesting the development of land that had traditionally been rented as allotments. The group devoted a great deal of time and effort to researching their position in law and were continually needing to make decisions about when and what they revealed to whom.

Although the matter was settled out of court eventually, the group could not afford to ultimately tell the developers everything they had learned as certain aspects of their findings undermined their own case. But the group chose to wait until the last couple of meetings with the developers and local authority officials to show much of their hand. This had the result of confusing the would-be developers, putting them on the back foot and in the end deciding to review their plans. The site, after four years, remained in use as allotments. In line with Che's contention that the guerrilla group is 'implacable' (relentless) in attack, the allotment group continued to develop their research about their rights and law with regard to the land.

Working with groups of this type is part and parcel of the youth worker's function in the community setting. Like the guerrilla, they have a role as a reformer or as Che had it 'a crusader for the people's freedom', always aiding local populations 'technically, economically, morally and culturally.' For Guevara, every effort needs to be made to establish co-operatives and to educate and inform the population. However, as importantly, the peasants will educate the guerrilla about the *reality* of their social condition, a reality which the guerrilla might only have known before in an abstract way.

The peasants can also provide practical lessons to the guerrillas, teaching them what reforms are most needed. The youth worker who draws back from taking on the task of educator, giving primacy to their own need to be educated by those they work with, for and among, has made a giant conceptual leap out of the ego trap in the training of professionals. Those who set out to educate a constituency by implication assume the relative ignorance of those people which is prejudice, stereotyping and discriminatory. For all we know, the areas we are based in are full of 'educated' people. How do I 'educate' a 65 year old who as a single mother raised six children? Coming from the most disadvantaged of backgrounds, she passed a social work degree at the age of 58! I didn't find any of this out until I had been working with her grandchildren for two years assuming that I was the main 'educator' in this family's life.

IT CAN HAPPEN ANYWHERE. REVOLUTION FEEDS UPON ITSELF

Guerrilla Warfare provides a step-by-step course in guerrilla methods and constantly repeats the same message; 'What has been done in Cuba can be done elsewhere, anywhere, whatever the odds.' Che maintained that the Cuban Revolution was not a unique event. It could happen almost anywhere. The basic factors were to be found elsewhere and if one factor was missing, another one would probably aid new guerrillas. The Cuban example was globally applicable.

Guevara insists that because only a few people are needed, a little equipment and his manual, together with determination to win, the odds can be overcome. What a relatively few Cubans did, all can do. Neither popular support nor a doctrine are necessary. If there is severe poverty, the severely poor will support the guerrillas as soon as they begin to operate. The fighting of a war of liberation will teach the guerrillas whatever lessons are the right ones for them. Revolution feeds upon itself.

Critics of *Guerrilla Warfare* have called the book 'wise after the event'. It seems to rationalize improvised responses to situations (I would argue that is exactly what youth workers do for much of the time). Che never denied this criticism, for analysis (something more questioning than reflection) is the rationalization of past success and failure. What he did deny was that the Cuban experience was a one-off and insular. He believed it to be something all the world could study and apply.

Fidel Castro said in his eulogy to Che on 18 October 1967:

> ... *When we think of Che, we do not think fundamentally of his military virtues. No! Warfare is a means and not an end. Warfare is a tool of revolutionaries. The important thing is the revolution, the revolutionary cause, revolutionary ideas, revolutionary objectives, revolutionary sentiments, revolutionary virtues.*

For the youth worker it is not the 'fight' or the 'struggle' that is of import (although these words are a romantic motivation for our work). Our thought, in the best of times, is applied to people finding a way to move forward into a better space that they identify as the place, that at a particular time, they want to go to and be in. This might involve more instinct than knowledge, more passion than education. In many ways none of that matters. Youth workers are essentially people who work with youth and learn from them and not essentially educators first and foremost.

It is probably the case that *Guerrilla Warfare* is only incidentally a manual. In the main, it provides a challenge to all activists in its three basic concepts, that
- *Popular forces can defeat armies*
- *The revolutionary focus can expand to create a total revolution*
  and
- *The revolution is to be won from the countryside.*

They are an open defiance of other theories that make concrete resources more crucial than the influence and authority of people. People are the main resource of the youth worker and nothing is more important and necessary for our work.

The Cuban revolutionaries won their war without the support of the Cuban (or any South American) Communist Party and long before they themselves turned to Communism as an ideology. This perhaps explains the most noticeable unorthodox element of *Guerrilla Warfare*. Che's Cuban experience made him preach the autonomy of the guerrilla group *outside* the central control of the monolithic Communist parties. This answered one of the questions that led to the break between the Anarchists and the Marxists in the 19th century – should a revolutionary struggle be directed by a central party organization or by those who are actually doing the fighting on the spot? This seems to underwrite for the youth worker the need to use and develop their professional judgment and be informed by those they are working with.

The nature of the everyday *guerrillero* is far from the starving, dirty, illiterate, fundamentalist or dangerous *desperado* lurking in the jungle to ambush and subvert. There is something in Che's concept of the guerrilla that is pertinent to all of us working on the borderlands betwixt liberty and exploitation, between lies and the chance to glimpse something of the glow of truth.

As Che once wrote:

For a soldier of the liberation, the best training is guerrilla life itself.
A leader who has not learned his difficult task in the daily exercise of
arms is not an authentic leader.

Guerrilla Warfare has been more immediately explosive than the *Communist Manifesto* was in its time. Following Che's writings and example, small handfuls of determined people have begun their own wars of liberation, sometimes choosing cities and universities in industrialised countries as battlegrounds rather than mountains and jungles.

According to Che, the small rebel group should fight, should win, with the support of the people. Governments and old parties, which have lost the support of the people, should be defeated or denied. The guerrilla makes the leader, the revolution makes itself.

YOUTH WORK – THE GUERRILLA PROFESSION

I have always thought of youth work as a 'guerrilla profession'. But the professional activity of youth workers is funded from the public purse, various sponsorships and bursaries from business interests and trust, bequests and individual donations. For an individual worker to decide that they will use those resources in a way that blatantly ignores or defies the type of direction that funding was specifically given to support is no more than a misappropriation of resources and tantamount to fraud. It is also a crassly unethical and immoral act of the over-inflated professional ego that causes one to believe they know is better for people than any other actual or potential stakeholder. At the same time to deliberately contradict agreed best practice, which is the resulting consensus of ones peers and colleagues, even if many have either refused or neglected to take part in the process of generating the same, is not romantic mutiny, the forgivable actions of a lovable rouge buccaneer, it is a form of professional treason and will, quite justly, likely be treated as such.

Youth workers, like guerrillas, have always been able to adapt to and make use of unfavourable environments and conditions with apparently inadequate resources. The successful guerrilla group is able to turn these seeming weaknesses into their strengths and the strength of youth work has historically been the same quality. The moment the profession is adequately resourced, which as a long term commitment would mean tens of billions of pounds of investment that would need to be diverted from other educational, health, housing or welfare provisions, it will no longer be youth work. Yes, things could always be better but in fact they are not and are unlikely to become better over the next decade or two. So we have our environment and we can make use of it.

Human beings, who are almost unique in having the ability to learn from the experience of others, are also remarkable for their apparent disinclination to do so – Douglas Adams

BIBLIOGRAPHY

Debray, R. (1975). *Che's Guerrilla war*. Penguin Books Ltd.
Guevara, E. (1969). *Guerrilla warfare*. Pelican.
Lewis, C. S. (2003). *The voyage of the dawn trader*. Index.
Montagu, A. (1952). *Mans most dangerous myth fallacy of race*. Columbia University Press.

CONCLUSION

When the revolution comes Jesus Christ is gonna be standing on the corner of Lenox Ave and 125th St trying to catch the first gypsy cab out of Harlem when the revolution comes When the revolution comes Some might even die before the revolution comes
— Abiodun Oyewole

The revolution will not be televised, will not be televised will not be televised, will not be televised. The revolution will be no re-run brothers; The revolution will be live
—Gil Scot-Heron

According to veteran Labour politician Tony Benn,

One of the most powerful weapons in the hands of the establishment, in its mission to control the people it governs, is to keep us in ignorance. Indeed, if information can be withheld. Presented selectively or adjusted to suit the interest of those at the top, a consensus will be constructed to suggest widespread support for what is being done or proposed. (cited in Powell 2001)

However, out of understanding arises purpose. Youth work, after becoming entangled, near strangled, in the doctrine of informal education, lost its way amid thickets of soundbites that few agreed with. This relative incomprehension caused purpose to fragment. But once examined these 'mottos' and 'one liners' mean little more than the tired and limiting conventions of education as a means of colonialism that spawned it. At present youth work is threatened with being devoured by what was once its tool.

Youth work has and does have meaning of itself and it has and can be understood as the extension of human kindness and collaboration, the sense we have for the protection and care of others – it is a socializing and humanizing influence, creative of civil society and something 'we' can use to build 'our' world for 'us' – all of 'us'.

We seek to work with people who want to turn their lives round – as such ours is a revolutionary pursuit. The Black Panther Party of Self Defence adopted the familiar phrase 'Power to the People' when they first came into being during the 1960s looking to forward the Civil Rights of Black people in America. However, they attached 'All the People' to this well known adage. If you think about it, those three words are as important as the first four. Democracy to be democracy has to be the 'rule of the people, by the people, for the people, all the people' – else it is just the tyranny of the many over the few and the creator of effectively de-politicised minorities. As such, the truly democratic social revolution will be achieved by the consensual will of 'all the people'. The youth worker's role is not to cause or agitate for revolution.

B. Belton, Developing Critical Youth Work Theory: Building Professional Judgment in the Community Context, 165–166.

We work not for any one cause of political position although those we work with might find some level of political enlightenment; we work 'for the people…all the people'. In that respect we are 'of the people' and (I'm going to use a 'must') we must never do anything that would hurt any of the people. We reflect them and they define what we are. But if we are professional, we refine who we are via the practice of our professional judgment – that is what this book has looked to be helpful with.

Kuwame Ture aka Stokely Carmichael, the founder of the idea and movement of 'Black Power', in the last years of his too short life finished the message on his answerphone with the expression 'Ready for the Revolution' – that's not a bad maxim for the youth worker may be?

As Che always knew, an idea can be more dangerous than a regiment. You now have some of his ideas; will you activate them in a way they will be passed on – 'Ready for the Revolution'?

Black power can be clearly defined for those who do not attach the fears of white America to their questions about it…Capitalism is a stupid system, a backward system… in order to understand white supremacy we must dismiss the fallacious notion that white people (the State via its professionals) *can* ('empower') *give anybody their freedom… No man can given anybody his freedom… the institutions that function in this country are clearly racist, and that they're built upon racism…The first need of a free people is to define their own terms* – Kwame Ture aka Stokely Carmichael

BIBLIOGRAPHY

Carmichael, S., & Hamilton, C. V. (1967). *Black power: The politics of liberation in America.* Vintage Books.

Powell, D. (2001). *Tony Benn a political life.* Continuum.

Lightning Source UK Ltd.
Milton Keynes UK
27 January 2011

166482UK00001B/29/P